The Alaskan
MUSHROOM HUNTER'S GUIDE

ALASKA NORTHWEST PUBLISHING COMPANY
Anchorage, Alaska

The Alaskan MUSHROOM HUNTER'S GUIDE

Ben Guild
Illustrations by Jack VanHoesen

Pleurotus (Panellus) serotinus

Text copyright © 1977 by Ben Guild.
Illustrations copyright © 1977 by Jack VanHoesen.
All rights reserved. No part of this book may be reproduced
or transmitted in any form or by any means, electronic
or mechanical, including photocopying, recording or by any
information storage and retrieval system, without
written permission of Alaska Northwest
Publishing Company.

Library of Congress cataloging in publication data:
Guild, Ben, 1924-
    The Alaskan mushroom hunter's guide.
    Bibliography: p.
    Includes index.
    1. Mushrooms—Alaska—Identification.
2. Cookery (Mushrooms) I. Title.
QK617.G84   589'.222'09798   76-29729
ISBN 0-88240-064-9

Design by Susan Hyde

Alaska Northwest Publishing Company
Box 4-EEE, Anchorage, Alaska 99509
Printed in U.S.A.

Leccinum insigne

To Susan

Contents

Preface ix
Chapter 1—Introduction 1
Chapter 2—What is a Mushroom? 3
Chapter 3—Mushroom Poisons 9
Chapter 4—Keys to the Mushrooms 13
Chapter 5—Gilled Mushrooms Part One—*Family Agaricaceae*
   With Spores Colorless, White, Cream, Yellow or Buff 33
     Genus *Amanita* 33
     Genus *Armillariella (Armillaria)* 40
     Genus *Cantharellus* 42
     Genus *Catathelasma* 44
     Genus *Clitocybe (Lyophyllum)* 46
     Genus *Collybia* 48
     Genus *Flammulina (Collybia)* 52
     Genus *Hygrophorus* 54
     Genus *Laccaria* 60
     Genus *Lactarius* 62
     Genus *Lepiota* 76
     Genus *Leucopaxillus (Clitocybe)* 78
     Genus *Limacella* 80
     Genus *Marasmius* 82
     Genus *Mycena* 86
     Genus *Pleurotus* 88
     Genus *Russula* 92
     Genus *Tricholoma* 106

Chapter 6—Gilled Mushrooms Part Two—*Family Agaricaceae*
   With Spores NOT Colorless, White, Cream, Yellow or Buff 117
     Genus *Clitopilus* 118
     Genus *Pluteus* 120
     Genus *Cortinarius* 122
     Genus *Gomphus (Neurophyllum)* 132
     Genus *Inocybe* 134
     Genus *Paxillus* 136
     Genus *Pholiota* 138

Genus *Agaricus* — 146
Genus *Naematoloma* — 154
Genus *Stropharia* — 156
Genus *Rozites* (*Pholiota*) — 158
Genus *Coprinus* — 160
Genus *Gomphidius* — 166

Chapter 7—Mushrooms Without Gills — 169
Fleshy Pore Fungi, Family *Boletaceae* — 170
Woody Pore Fungi, Family *Polyporaceae* — 186
Toothed, or Hedgehog, Fungi, Family *Hydnaceae* — 194
Club, or Coral, Fungi, Family *Clavariaceae* — 202
Sac, or Sponge, Fungi, Family *Helvellaceae* — 216
Puffballs, or Stomach Fungi, Family *Lycoperdaceae* — 228
Cup Fungi, Family *Pezizaceae* — 234
Earth Tongues, Family *Geoglossaceae* — 240

Chapter 8—Mushrooms as Food — 243
Mushrooms and Nutrition — 243
The Pick of the Mushroom Crop — 245
Preserving Mushrooms — 245
Cooking With Mushrooms — 247
Hors d'Oeuvres, Spreads and Relishes — 248
Soups and Stocks — 249
Salads and Dressings — 252
Sauces and Gravies — 253
Light Meals — 255
Omelets and Souffles — 256
Fried Mushrooms — 257
Creamed Mushrooms — 258
Broiled and Baked Dishes — 259
Stuffed Mushrooms — 264
Mushroom Specialties — 265

Chapter 9—Field Notes — 269
Statistical Summary — 269
A Form for Field Notes — 271
Check Lists — 272

Glossary — 279

Bibliography — 281

Index — 283

Preface

After the immense grandeur of the Alaskan landscape, two things impressed me most when I came to Alaska. One was the great profusion of plant and animal life around me. The other was the very limited literature covering the natural and biological life of the state.

Compared to what has been written about the natural history of the lower 48 states and the rest of North America, information on Alaska is scanty. And plants, especially the lower plants, seem to have suffered lack of recognition most of all.

Frontier Alaskans (that means all Alaskans) enjoy gathering wild foods, including mushrooms, and they do so almost at will and fancy. Until now, however, mushroom hunters have not had a good Alaskan field guide to help them distinguish the edible mushrooms from the few that would sicken or poison them. This book is offered to fill that need; it is my contribution to the mushroom hunters of Alaska.

The book will be useful for other areas of western North America if allowance is made for shifts in form and color.

I am indebted to Dr. Daniel E. Stuntz, of the University of Washington, for his review and criticism of the manuscript. My thanks also to mycophagist Cheryl Workman, whose contributions to mushroom cookery are excelled only by her enthusiasm in gathering the wild foods of Alaska. Good hunting and good eating.

Morchella esculenta

Figure 1 — The Regions of Alaska

Chapter 1
Introduction

This book is written for the amateur mushroom hunters of Alaska. It is a technical book only from the standpoint of providing proper scientific names and precise descriptions of the mushrooms. The common names are given also.

Of the more than 7,000 species of fleshy fungi (mushrooms) in the world, about half grow abundantly in North America, and 500 of these are found in Alaska. Most are edible; a few others are inedible, dangerous or poisonous, and of some the edibility is yet unknown.

I have tried to point out about 100 of the more common species, ones that are readily seen and easily found. About three-fourths of them are considered edible, so you should have plenty to choose from.

We will be concerned mainly with the mushrooms of the Southcentral region of Alaska (see Figure 1), an area of about 200,000 square miles. Many of the mushrooms found here are also found in other areas of Alaska, especially in Southeastern Alaska, in the northern extremes of Western Alaska and Kodiak Island, and in the southern part of the Interior.

Southcentral Alaska, an area of warm summers and moderately cold winters, fans out above the Gulf of Alaska. From the northern edge of the Aleutian Range in the west, it extends eastward along the southern edge of the great Alaska Range to the Canadian border; it includes the Kenai Peninsula and the Talkeetna, Wrangell, and Chugach Mountains. Anchorage is the largest city.

The growing season is approximately 120 days; rainfall averages 17 to 20 inches a year. Most of the state's agricultural land is located in this area.

This is a land of coniferous forests, predominantly spruce and juniper, as well as scattered hemlock, fir and tamarack. The most abundant deciduous trees and shrubs are birch, willow, poplar, cottonwood, aspen and alder.

A great many shrubs and wild flowers grow in Alaska, and this area—being one of the most temperate in climate—has an abundance of wild plants to delight collectors and lovers of wild flowers.

Mushrooms grow abundantly all over Southcentral, especially in the southern region along creek banks, in bogs and meadows, and on the lower slopes of the mountains. They grow over most of the Kenai Peninsula and the great Copper River and Chitina River valleys.

Each species of mushroom has its own manner of growth, called habit, as well as its natural place of growth, called habitat. Many grow individually on the ground or on wood; others grow in bunchlike clusters. Many mushrooms grow with a particular species of tree or shrub and are found nowhere else. Generally you can find more than one of a species in any location. But many times you will find two or more different species growing in the same area, and positive identification of each becomes very important.

Photographs that you might take of mushrooms are a good aid to identification and make an interesting record of your collections. Perhaps you will want to keep a log or notebook to record your finds for future gathering. The chapter on field notes at the back of this book suggests a form useful for that purpose.

Become acquainted with others who gather mushrooms and form a group to reinforce the knowledge of mushroom hunting and cookery. Learn to use as many reference books as you can to increase your skill as a collector of wild mushrooms.

Chapter 2
What is a Mushroom?

Mushroom is the common name for the fruiting body, or sporophore, of a group of primitive plants called fungi. The fungi are nongreen plants; that is, they have no chlorophyll. Chlorophyll is the green substance present in all higher forms of plant life that enables the green plants to manufacture their own food.

Fungi are either saprophytes, living on dead and decaying vegetative matter, or parasites, deriving their sustenance from living things. We will be concerned only with the saprophytic fungi and their fruiting bodies, which we call mushrooms.

Growth and Structure

To better understand the mushroom's structure, we should know something about how it grows. Like most plants, a mushroom has a root system—or something like other root systems. It is a network of white fibrous material, almost filamentous, called mycelium. Mycelium is present in soil just under the surface, and it exists all through decaying forest humus, dead trees, stumps and logs. When the temperature, moisture and light are right, little buds appear and grow into the fruiting bodies (see figure 2, page 4).

4   What Is a Mushroom?

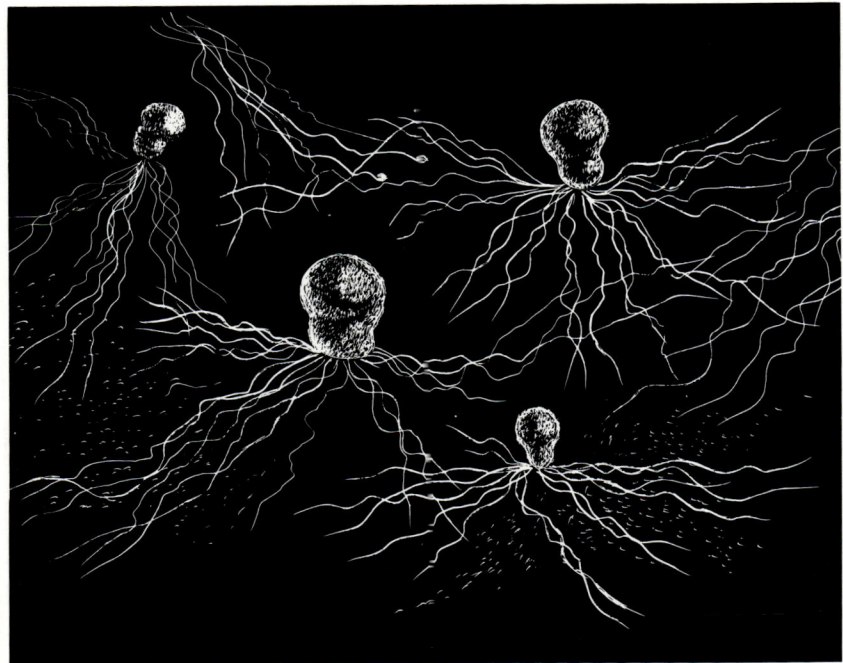

Figure 2—Mycelium With the Buds of a Gilled Mushroom

As the mushroom matures, structures that have a great deal to do with future generations and perpetuation of the species develop within.

Mushrooms have only two major parts above ground, or above whatever material they're growing from, and they are readily seen. The two parts are the stem (stipe) and the cap (pileus). Many species, such as the gilled, fleshy pore, toothed, sponge and earth tongue fungi, have clearly defined stems and caps. Other fungi, such as the woody pore shelf fungi, the club or coral fungi, the puffballs and the cup fungi, have fruiting bodies with varying not-mushroomlike shapes.

Stem

In some mushrooms, the stem is so short as to appear absent; many have no stems at all and are said to be sessile. In others the stems take on all kinds of forms and shapes, from long and thin to short and fat or bulbous. Some stems are fleshy, some hollow and fibrous, some brittle, some slimy. Most mushrooms grow singly, but some are clustered; and some have the remains of a covering veil as a ring (annulus) high on the stem and a jagged cup (volva) at the base, or both. Figure 3 shows the development of a typical gilled mushroom.

Cap

The caps of mushrooms differ, and there is a great variety of shapes, sizes and forms in the typical mushroom types (see Figure 3). The gilled fungi have a series of flat platelike structures underneath, radiating from the stem outward, called lamellae (gills), which in many species are distinctive.

Some caps are dry; others are sticky, powdery, shiny or scaly. Most are colored from whitish to dark brown, or have a blackish tinge; but some are a vivid red, or orange or yellow. Some are slimy always, and some are slimy only when wet. Some exude a milky juice of various colors when wounded or broken; and some change color when creased, bruised or cut.

Most caps are convex when young, becoming flattened as the plant matures. Some are depressed in the center, while others may have a knob (umbo) on the top. Some caps are funnel-form. Others are convoluted and folded, pitted and ridged, spiny, warty or smooth. The edges of caps may be smooth, wavy, lobed, toothed or split.

The color, size, shape and form of the caps are some of the best characteristics to use to identify mushrooms. However, keep in mind that

Figure 3—Development of a Typical Gilled Mushroom, One of the Amanitas

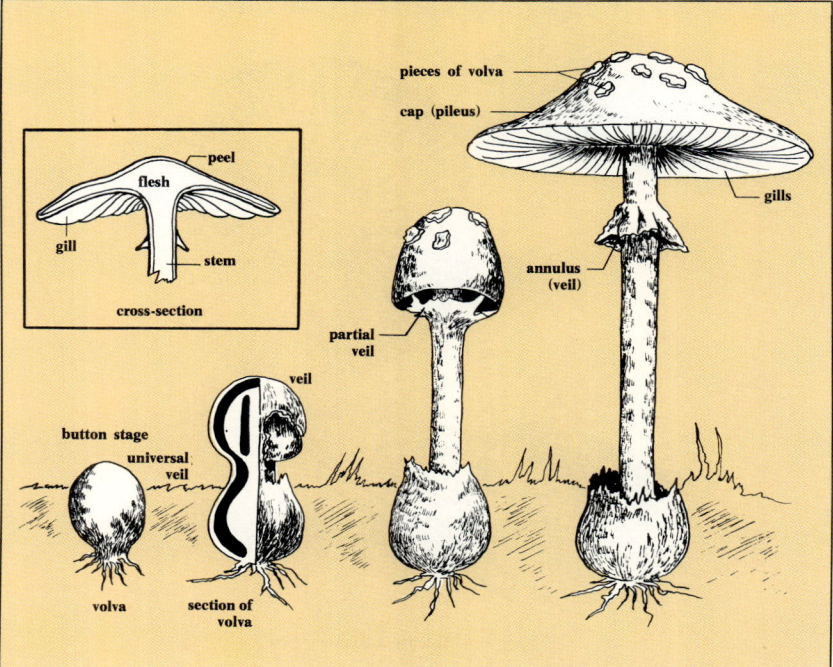

the color of the cap is not a valid check in itself, because exposure to extensive sunlight or abundant rainfall, or both, tends to bleach out many mushrooms. A good example is *Amanita muscaria,* the poisonous fly agaric. In its natural form, this mushroom's cap is reddish orange; in exposed areas, however, you will find caps that are light orange and yellowish to almost white. This bleaching or decoloration of a mushroom does not take away any dangerous properties it may have.

Spore Color

Many mushrooms have a distinctive spore color, which ranges from hyaline (colorless) through white, yellow, brown, purple and black. The spore color is one of the best aids in the identification of any mushroom. A spore print should be made of every species collected if possible.

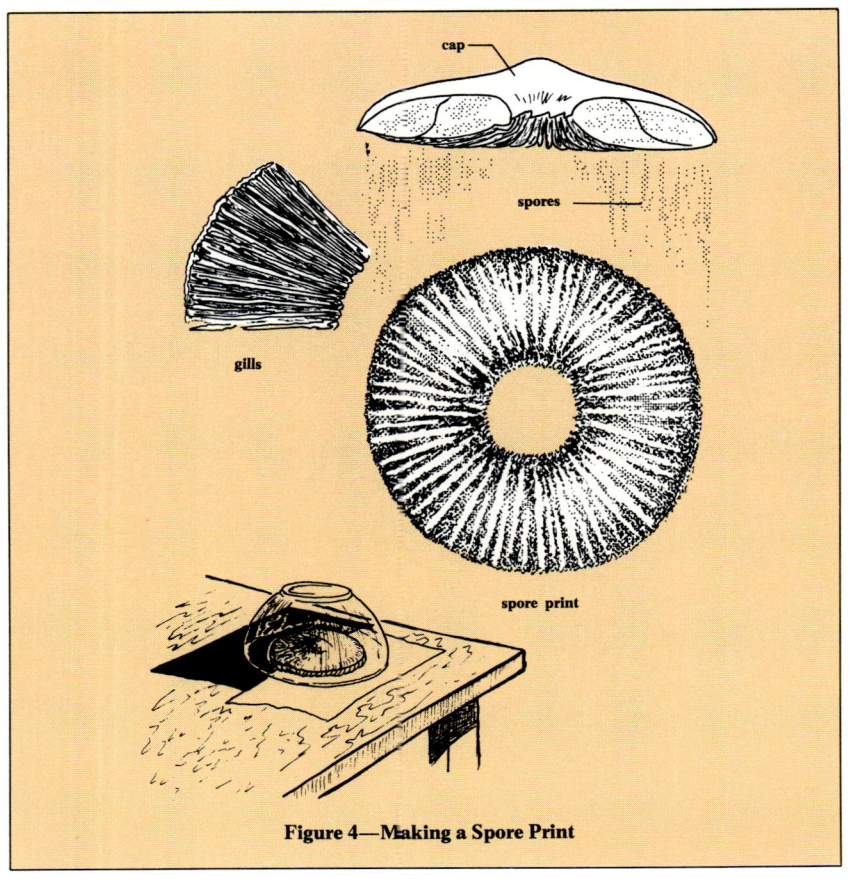

Figure 4—Making a Spore Print

To make a spore print, place the cap of a mature mushroom on construction paper with gills or pores down (see Figure 4). Be sure you have cut or broken the stem so the cap will lie flat. Cover the cap with a large bowl or dish and leave it for a few hours to overnight in a room at normal temperature. Take care not to move or otherwise disturb the mushroom so the spore print will be sharp and clear. When removing the cap, lift straight up so as not to rub across the spore pattern. These spore prints may be sprayed with a fixative lacquer, and after drying will be set enough to file in your records. Use black paper for the mushrooms with the light-colored spores and white paper for those with darker spores. Or use two sheets, one of each color, spliced together so that the mushroom lies across the dividing line. The spore color and pattern will be seen regardless of the coloration.

No matter how you do it, it is advisable to know the spore color of any mushroom that you are trying to identify.

It is these spores, millions of spores, dropping from the mature mushroom that are carried by wind and water and on the feet of birds and animals to places of favorable habitat; there they germinate into the mycelium and start the process all over again.

What Is a Toadstool?

Toadstool is nothing more than an old folk tale name given to inedible mushrooms and to those thought to be poisonous. This is really a misnomer, because to the untrained mushroom hunter, all unidentified mushrooms are toadstools, whether edible or poisonous.

Poisonous?

There have been many so-called tests that were supposed to tell if a mushroom was poisonous or not. Most of these are just folk tales. At one time it was thought that stirring cooking mushrooms with a silver spoon or inserting a silver coin was a sure-fire test. If the spoon or coin turned black the mushrooms were poisonous; if not, then the mushrooms were good to eat. I'm sure this fallacy has led many an experimenter to a violent death. The only test for an edible or poisonous mushroom is positive identification. *If you can't identify it, don't eat it.* Even edible mushrooms can disagree with one's digestion, just as fruits and vegetables do; strawberries and other foods sometimes cause allergies. It is wise to not eat too much of a species the first time you try it. Never eat a mushroom raw until you know what it is; taste it if you wish, but do not swallow. Some mushrooms have a very distinctive taste—bitter, peppery or garliclike and can be identified this way; but sometimes even edible mushrooms eaten raw can cause gastric disturbances.

Mature or old mushrooms are often found to be infested with insect larvae and are thus inedible or at least unpalatable to most of us.

When you pick mushrooms, never put more than one kind in the same container. If you wish to gather more than one kind, keep them separated in their own containers. Small plastic bags are ideally suited to mushroom gathering. Remember that even a small piece of a poisonous mushroom will taint all the rest, especially in cooking.

Learn the distinguishing features of a few good edible mushrooms and stick to gathering those species for your table. Never experiment with an unknown species to see what will happen; you may be unlucky.

The "foolproof four" mushrooms might be a good place for a new mushroomer to start. They are edible, readily available mushrooms that are almost impossible to mistake for any other kind. C. M. Christensen, who called them "foolproof" in the 1940's, saw only four; the species classifications we now use give us six:

Species
    64. *Coprinus comatus,* shaggy mane, page 162.
    75. *Laetiporus (Polyporus) sulphureus,* sulphur shelf, page 188.
    92. *Morchella angusticeps,* conic morel, page 222.
    93. *Morchella esculenta,* sponge morel, page 224.
    95. *Calvatia gigantea,* giant puffball, page 228.
    96. *Lycoperdon perlatum,* gem-studded puffball, page 230.

Be sure to use the keys (Chapter 4) to identify them; that's not a step to be skipped.

Chapter 3
Mushroom Poisons

There are comparatively few poisonous mushrooms in relation to the total number of species known to exist in the world. However, it is these few that cause the most problems.

There is only one way to differentiate between the edible and poisonous fungi: Learn to recognize them and identify them beyond any question.

Most toxic species are not fatal to healthy adults, but produce effects such as heart palpitations or nausea, act as a laxative, induce hallucinations or intoxication or severe sweating, or a combination of some of these symptoms.

A few mushrooms have toxins that are deadly to man; others affect the central nervous system with severe results.

There appear to be at least six major groups of toxins now known to occur in the fungi. I will list them briefly in the order of their severity, with the most deadly listed first.

Group A: Phallotoxins and Amatoxins

Some of the species producing Group A poisons may taste quite good. Several hours may elapse after the toxin enters the bloodstream before the faster acting phallotoxins are converted by liver enzymes into a compound that begins to attack and destroy liver cells. After the long, latent period the victim suffers extreme pain, severe vomiting and diarrhea. Several hours later the slower acting amatoxin is felt, and during the interim the victim may feel somewhat better. However, the onset of severe pain resumes, then continues from 4 to 6 days and often results in the death of the person. If a person does survive the ordeal, the effects may last for several weeks and may result in partial necrosis of some liver cells.

Mushroom species known to have toxins in Group A are: *Amanita verna, A. virosa, A. bisporigera, A. tenuifolia* and *A. phalloides,* as well as *Galerina marginata, G. autumnalis* and *G. venenata.* None of these mushrooms are common in Alaska and some of them may not grow here at all, but they are often found in other parts of North America and the rest of the world, and we should be aware of them.

Group B: Muscarine

This toxin excites the parasympathetic nervous system to slow the heart, dilate blood vessels and constrict the pupils of the eyes. Atropine is used to counteract the effects of muscarine; recovery in healthy individuals is usually rapid.

Mushrooms known to have toxins of Group B are: *Inocybe patouillardi, I. napipes, I. fastigiata* and many other species of *Inocybe, Clitocybe dealbata* and *Amanita muscaria,* from which muscarine was first isolated. Only traces of muscarine occur in *A. muscaria* and *A. pantherina,* and probably several other species of *Amanita,* as well as in *Hebeloma crustuliniforme.*

Group C: Muscimol, Ibotenic Acid and Other Related Compounds

These act on the central nervous system. They, and not muscarine, comprise the chief toxins in *Amanita muscaria,* but the amounts of muscimol and ibotenic acid vary markedly with the geographic location of that species. When large amounts of either *A. muscaria* or *A. pantherina,* with high content of the two toxins, are eaten, a severe illness results that could be dangerous to the very old, the very young, or generally unhealthy persons. Healthy adults usually recover with no aftereffects.

Mushrooms known to have the toxins of Group C are: *Amanita muscaria* and *A. pantherina.*

Group D: Psilocybin and Psilocin

These are well-known hallucinogenic compounds. They have a strong, long-lasting effect on the central nervous system, producing visions and optical distortions and hindering normal sensations. The quantity eaten and the personality, mood and physiological condition of the person are involved in the total effect. If eaten by children these mushrooms could have deleterious effects. It is not yet known if there are other toxic properties present in addition to the hallucinogenic poisons.

Mushrooms known to have toxins in Group D are: *Psilocybe cubensis, P. fimentaria, P. mexicana, P. semilanceata, P. caerulescens, Conocybe cyanescens, C. cyanopus* and certain geographic or chemical races of *Panaeolus foenisecii.*

Group E: Gyromitrin Toxins

Gyromitrin (monomethyl hydrazine, MMH) is a protoplasmic toxin that in large enough doses can be fatal. Symptoms include diarrhea, vomiting and loss of muscle coordination. Severe headaches and body pains may last for some time. The toxic reaction varies with the amount of the mushroom eaten, the method of cooking and the individual's tolerance to gyromitrin. There have been several fatalities in Europe from eating this mushroom, and some cases of poisoning have been recorded from the area of North America east of the Rocky Mountains. Since gyromitrin is both volatile at temperatures around 100° C and soluble in hot water, a preliminary parboiling followed by thorough cooking is recommended for all the mushrooms listed in the next paragraph.

Mushrooms known to have toxins in Group E are: *Gyromitra (Helvella) esculenta, G. fastigiata* and *G. brunnea*.

Group F: Gastrointestinal and Other Toxins

There are several toxins of as yet unknown structure that occur in mushrooms, but are rarely fatal. They act mainly as purgatives, causing diarrhea, nausea and vomiting. Eating large quantities of mushrooms containing these toxins might be dangerous for old persons, young children or individuals whose health is greatly deteriorated to start with. Healthy adults, however, should recover without any lasting aftereffects. Mushrooms containing toxins of Group F comprise the largest number of species of poisonous mushrooms, and the list is not yet complete.

Some of the mushrooms known to have toxins of Group F are: *Entoloma lividum, E. strictium, Hebeloma crustuliniforme* and other *Hebeloma* species, *Lactarius rufus, L. torminosus, L. uvidus, Chlorophyllum molybdites (Lepiota morgani), Marasmius urens, Omphalotus illudens, Ramaria (Clavaria) formosa, Russula emetica, R. fragilis* and *Tricholoma pardinum*.

Special Cases

Coprinus atramentarius is normally an edible mushroom except when eaten while imbibing any alcoholic beverage. Sometimes, and with some individuals, the consumption of alcohol within 72 hours before or after eating this mushroom will bring on the symptoms of palpitations of the heart and flushing of the skin, with extreme discomfort. These effects generally last only a few hours or less, and recovery is rapid unless more mushrooms and alcohol are consumed.

Mushroom hunters in Alaska should be especially cautious in sampling the golden pholiota, *Pholiota aurea*. Wells and Kempton reported in 1965 that several people in the region around Anchorage had unpleasant gastrointestinal upset from eating *Pholiota aurea* whereas others who ate the same mushroom were unaffected by it. The same results have been reported recently in western Washington. The fact that this fungus is said to be edible and excellent in almost all current handbooks shows the necessity for being very careful when trying any mushrooms for the first time. Eat only a small amount, in the hopes of being only slightly sick if the mushroom is going to affect you adversely.

What to Do

Any time you think you have eaten a poisonous mushroom, you should purge the stomach immediately and see a doctor as soon as possible.

It always helps to have at least a small piece, if not the whole specimen, of the fungus in question along to facilitate diagnosis.

There are many good, wholesome, edible species of mushrooms in Alaska, and you should have no trouble finding those that are harmless.

Chapter 4
Keys to the Mushrooms

In Alaska there are perhaps 500 species of mushrooms, many of which differ only slightly from one another in appearance. In this book, we describe only the 101 most common and useful species. This means that many of the keys could lead to a species different from, but closely resembling, the one intended. It is important, therefore, that you always compare your specimen carefully with both the description and the species illustration before deciding that your identification is correct.

The keys given in this chapter provide a systematic method for identifying a mushroom. A process of elimination takes the mushroom hunter from all mushrooms to one mushroom, from family to genus to species. Each step of the process consists of an opposing pair of descriptive statements requiring a choice to be made—It's this (a) or that (b). Each step narrows the investigation.

To use the keys, compare your mushroom with the first statement; if it agrees, go to the key number given at the end of the statement. If your mushroom does not agree with the first statement, compare it with the second statement, and if it agrees, go to the key number given at the end of that statement. Follow the sequence of key numbers until the genus is established; continue through the species descriptions until you reach the one that matches your mushroom.

Begin with the keys to families.

KEYS TO FAMILIES

I. Mushrooms with flat, platelike lamellae (gills) underneath the cap radiating from the stem or their point of attachment outward→gilled mushrooms (agarics), family *Agaricaceae*, key 1.

II. Mushrooms without gills:
 a. Fruiting body mushroomlike, soft and fleshy, with cap and stem, the caps having a series of closely packed tubes or pores underneath→fleshy pore fungi, family *Boletaceae*, key 33.
 b. Fruiting body growing on wood as shelflike brackets with closely packed tubes or pores underneath, firm when young, becoming woody, corky and tough when old→woody pore fungi, family *Polyporaceae*, key 40.
 c. Fruiting body either mushroomlike, with cap and stem, the caps having crowded, soft, spinelike teeth covering the under surface, or else consisting of a mass of fleshy branches growing on wood, with downward-pointing spines clustered along the branches→toothed, or hedgehog, fungi, family *Hydnaceae*, key 43.
 d. Fruiting body either a corallike mass of erect, fleshy branches, or a simple, erect, club-shaped or spindle-shaped structure that is not divided into cap and stem→club, or coral, fungi, family *Clavariaceae*, key 46.
 e. Fruiting body consisting of a definite cap borne on a stem, the cap with a wrinkled or convoluted surface, or spongelike and pitted→sac, or sponge, fungi, famliy *Helvellaceae*, key 53.
 f. Fruiting body a sessile pear-shaped or globose structure with a definite, often tough outer rind or shell, and a white, pulpy interior resembling fine-textured styrofoam, that eventually becomes transformed into a dry, powdery mass of spores→puffballs, or stomach fungi, family *Lycoperdaceae*, key 58.
 g. Fruiting body a cup-shaped or saucer-shaped structure, with thin, brittle walls, and with the spore-bearing surface lining the interior of the cup→cup fungi, family *Pezizaceae*, key 60.
 h. Fruiting body a small, erect, spatulalike structure growing on leaf mold and mosses→earth tongues, family *Geoglossaceae*, key 62.

KEYS TO THE GILLED MUSHROOMS (FAMILY AGARICACEAE)

1. a. Spores white, cream color, yellow, or buff→key 5.
   b. Spores not white, cream color, yellow, or buff→key 2.

2. a. Spores pink or brownish salmon color→key 24.
   b. Spores not pink or brownish salmon color→key 3.

3. a. Spores purple-brown, reddish chocolate, or blackish purple→key 25.
   b. Spores either some shade of brown, without any purple shades, or black→key 4.

4. a. Spores yellow-brown, grayish brown, cigar brown, umber, rusty brown, etc., without any purple tones→key 27.
   b. Spores black or brownish black→key 32.

5. a. Either a volva present or an annulus present, or both volva and annulus present→key 6.
   b. Neither volva nor annulus present→key 10.

6. a. Annulus present, volva absent→key 7.
   b. Volva present, annulus present or absent→genus *AMANITA*.

   A. Cap red to scarlet, orange, or yellow, fading to nearly whitish on exposed areas, covered with thick, whitish to buff, floccose warts; annulus present, white to cream color→species 1, *Amanita muscaria*.

   B. Cap grayish brown with slight purplish tinge, smooth, usually having a few remnants of the crumbling gray volva on the margin; annulus present, gray→species 2, *Amanita porphyria*.

   C. Cap whitish, tawny, brown, or gray, usually smooth or may have remnants of the volva; margin grooved-striate, annulus lacking→species 3, *Amanita (Amanitopsis) vaginata*.

7. a. Annulus double, two distinct rings separated by a short length of stem→genus *CATATHELASMA*.

   A. Gills decurrent. Cap large, thick-fleshed, whitish to smoky gray, slightly viscid when wet, drying dull and smooth→species 6, *Catathelasma imperialis*.

   b. Annulus single (only one ring)→key 8.

8. a. Cap viscid. Stem viscid below the annulus→genus *LIMACELLA*.

   A. Cap egg-shaped, becoming campanulate then flattened with age, umbonate, glutinous, pale yellowish at the center. Gills free, white. Stem viscid below the annulus, silky above→species 24, *Limacella illinita*.

   b. Neither cap nor stem viscid→key 9.

9. a. Gills attached, often decurrent→genus *ARMILLARIELLA (ARMILLARIA)*.

   A. Cap acorn-shaped to round, then flattened to convex, sometimes subumbonate, yellow-buff, yellow-brown, or rusty tinged, minutely scaled with dark tufts of fibrils, margin striate. Gills subdecurrent, whitish becoming rusty brown. In dense clusters at the base of living trees and old stumps→species 4, *Armillariella (Armillaria) mellea.*

   b. Gills free—genus *LEPIOTA*.

   A. Cap acorn-shaped at first, covered with a thin layer of buff-yellow or brownish tissue, expanding to convex-campanulate, outer tissue breaking into scales, the umbo smooth, margin often ragged with veil fragments. Gills free, white. Edges woolly→species 22, *Lepiota clypeolaria.*

10. a. Cap, stem, and gills NOT exuding a milky juice where cut→key 11.
    b. Cap, stem, and gills exuding white or colored milky juice where cut→genus *LACTARIUS*.

    A. Cap whitish to flesh colored, stained with brown spots, viscid. Gills decurrent, pink. Latex white, acrid→species 15, *Lactarius controversus.*

    B. Cap reddish orange, zoned, becoming grayish or gray-green where bruised or with age, viscid when wet. Latex orange, mild→species 16, *Lactarius deliciosus.*

    C. Cap gray or putty color or brownish, viscid, smooth, not zoned, stem viscid, same color as cap, gills white. Latex white, drying greenish to bluish gray, acrid→species 17, *Lactarius mucidus.*

    D. Cap dull yellow, viscid, hairy, not zoned, margin inrolled at first and very hairy or woolly; all parts becoming purple where bruised or cut. Latex white, becoming lilac upon exposure→species 18, *Lactarius representaneus.*

    E. Cap bay-red to rufous, not fading with age, dry, not zoned, stem same color as cap, gills paler than cap. Latex white, unchanging, very acrid→species 19, *Lactarius rufus.*

F. Cap pale yellow to brownish yellow, zoned, viscid, slightly to densely hairy at margin. Gills whitish. Stem yellow, with shallow pits. Latex white, quickly changing to sulphur yellow, acrid→species 20, *Lactarius scrobiculatus*.

G. Cap pale yellow-buff to rosy flesh color, often with deeply colored zones, viscid, smooth at center, margin inrolled with long, persistent, woolly hairs. Latex white, unchanging, very acrid→species 21, *Lactarius torminosus*.

11. a. Flesh of cap or stem or both showing evidence of a fibrous nature when broken (NOTE: take this choice for small, fragile mushrooms with membranous cap and stem 1/8 inch or less thick); size and color of the fruiting body varies→key 12.
    b. Flesh of cap and stem where broken having a granular surface like chalk or Swiss cheese, without any evidence of a fibrous nature. Moderate- to large-size mushrooms with the caps usually (but not always) brightly colored in red, yellow, purple, green or bluish→genus *RUSSULA*.

    A. Cap dull to dark smoky green, darker in center, sometimes tinged brownish, paler on margin, viscid when wet, velvety when dry, fragile, margin even at first, becoming striate with age→species 30, *Russula aeruginea*.

    B. Cap white, slightly woolly, staining brown, margin not striate. Gills decurrent, sometimes forked, white, staining cinnamon or brown where bruised or with age. Stem whitish with brown stains→species 31, *Russula brevipes*.

    C. Cap bright chrome yellow, margin slightly striate, flesh whitish turning gray where bruised; associated with birch trees→species 32, *Russula claroflava (flava)*.

    D. Cap dull whitish, becoming smoky brown, slightly viscid, smooth. Gills whitish, becoming reddish where bruised, then turning black. Flesh white turning reddish then black where bruised→species 33, *Russula densifolia*.

    E. Cap rosy to blood red, fading with age to whitish, viscid when wet, smooth, shining; peel separates readily; margin strongly striated. Flesh white, red under the peel, fragile. Taste very peppery→species 34, *Russula emetica*.

F. Cap yellowish to dingy brown, smooth, viscid, margin coarsely striated. Gills whitish, becoming yellowish with age, dingy brownish where bruised, exuding water drops when young. Odor strong, nauseous→species 35, *Russula foetens*.

G. Cap reddish purple to olive-green (olivaceous) in center, viscid when wet, smooth when dry, margin even, peel difficult to separate from flesh of cap. Odor of fish or crab with age or upon drying. Stem flushed with rose color, staining brown where handled→species 36, *Russula xerampelina*.

12. a. Gills with blunt, obtusely rounded edges, or reduced to a series of veins or blunt ridges→key 13.
    b. Gills of the normal type, bladelike with sharp edges→key 14.

13. a. Stem lacking, or very short if present. Veins or ridges lavender or purple→genus *GOMPHUS* (*NEUROPHYLLUM*).

    A. Cap light purple to faded purplish brown, flat to club-shaped, thick-fleshed, dry. Veins or ridges blunt, thick, interconnected by cross-veins, decurrent, frequently forked, purplish→species 49, *Gomphus clavatus* (*Neurophyllum clavatum*).

    b. Stem long and slender, cap thin-fleshed, gills ridgelike, blunt-edged, yellowish to grayish→genus *CANTHARELLUS*.

    A. Cap brownish yellow to ochraceous, depressed, somewhat infundibuliform, slightly hairy-silky, margin irregular and wavy→species 5, *Cantharellus tubaeformis*.

14. a. Stem well developed, at or near the center of the cap. Fruiting bodies growing on wood or on the ground→key 16.
    b. Stem lacking, cap fastened by one side to wood→key 15.

15. a. Cap white, dry, fan-shaped, in clusters on conifer wood→genus *PLEUROTUS*.

    A. Cap white, watery, slightly striated on margin, laterally attached, always on wood in dense overlapping clusters→species 28, *Pleurotus* (*Pleurotellus*) *porrigens*.

    b. Cap olivaceous, yellow-green or dull brown; slimy-viscid when wet; singly or clustered on hardwood logs→genus *PLEUROTUS* (*PANELLUS*).

A. Cap semicircular to kidney-shaped, attached by a yellowish velvety tubercle visible only from below→species 29, *Pleurotus (Panellus) serotinus*.

16. a. Cap brown, viscid, stem velvety, fruiting bodies in clusters of wood→genus *FLAMMULINA (COLLYBIA)*.

    A. Cap yellowish to reddish brown, smooth. Gills yellowish. Stem bright cinnamon. Fruiting bodies growing in dense clusters on hardwood→species 10, *Flammulina (Collybia) velutipes*.

    b. Not with the combination of features given in the above key entry→key 17.

17. a. Cap, gills, and stem lavender or grayish lilac, moist, soft and fragile; crushed flesh with odor of radish→genus *MYCENA*.

    A. Cap pale rose to violet, sometimes grayish violet to nearly white, glabrous, moist, translucent-striate on margin. Gills adnate, interveined, close, tinged with the color of the cap. Stem sometimes twisted and striated, hollow, same color as the cap→species *Mycena pura*.

    b. Fruiting body not uniformly lavender or grayish lilac; crushed flesh not with a radish odor→key 18.

18. a. Cap at least 1/2 inch wide, usually much wider. Stem more than 1/16 inch thick, varying in consistency→key 19.
    b. Cap less than 1/2 inch in diameter, membranous. Stem about 1/16 inch thick, tubular, tough and pliable→genus *MARASMIUS*.

    A. Caps very small, reddish brown to purplish tinged, radiately wrinkled, smooth. Gills adnate, buff or flesh color. Stems tubular, tough, blackish; growing on conifer needles→species 25, *Marasmius androsaceus*.

    B. Caps very small, white slightly umbilicate, wrinkled, smooth. Gills adnate, distant, white. Stem red-brown, whitish at the top, hairy at the base→species 26, *Marasmius epiphyllus*.

19. a. Cap and stem reddish brown or tawny. Gills thick, waxy, pink. Stem tough, fibrous→genus *LACCARIA*.

A. Cap color varies from reddish brown to flesh or pallid. Cap slightly umbilicate, smooth at first then somewhat scaly, hygrophanous→species 14, *Laccaria laccata*.

b. Fruiting body not having all the features mentioned in the preceding key entry→key 20.

20. a. Stem stout, fleshy or pulpy, or soft and fragile, breaking readily when bent→key 21.
b. Stem slender, cartilaginous, often hollow, pliable, tending to split lengthwise when bent→genus *COLLYBIA*.

A. Cap reddish to vinaceous brown, smooth, watery, margin pale, fading to nearly whitish. Gills free to adnexed, crowded, whitish or with reddish tinge. Stem reddish to vinaceous brown, smooth above, whitish-hairy below. Fruiting bodies growing in dense clusters on wood or from the base of stumps→species 8, *Collybia acervata*.

B. Cap yellowish to reddish tan, fading with age, smooth, moist when fresh. Gills adnate to adnexed, narrow, crowded, whitish to pallid. Stem same color as the cap, often tufted at the base with white mycelium. Fruiting bodies not growing in dense clusters from wood→species 9, *Collybia dryophila*.

21. a. Gills not markedly thicker at the base (where attached to the cap) than at the edge. Cap neither red and conic nor blackening. Stem not viscid (but the cap may be)→key 22.
b. Gills thick at the base, narrowly triangular in cross section. Either the cap is red and conic and blackening, or both cap and stem are viscid→genus *HYGROPHORUS*.

A. Cap conic and remaining so, orange, red-orange or yellowish, tinged with olive to blackish streaks, blackening when bruised or with age, viscid when wet, drying silky, margin often splits as cap expands, sometimes lobed. Gills pallid, yellowish. Flesh tinged orange. Stem yellowish to orange tinged, blackening where bruised, readily splitting lengthwise→species 11, *Hygrophorus conicus*.

B. Cap white with yellow flecks or granules, viscid when fresh. Gills decurrent, white. Stem viscid when fresh, whitish, sprinkled with yellow granules that may form a yellow annular zone→species 12, *Hygrophorus chrysodon*.

C. Cap white, glutinous subumbonate, margin slightly woolly and incurved. Stem equally glutinous, white, dotted at the top with small scales→species 13, *Hygrophorus eburneus*.

22. a. Fruiting bodies growing on the ground in dense clusters of many individuals. Cap soapy feeling (but not viscid), beige or buff or gray→ genus *CLITOCYBE* (*LYOPHYLLUM*).

    A. Cap tinged with buff or gray, moist, smooth, convex, often irregular in outline. Gills adnate, close, narrowing at each end, whitish. Fruiting bodies growing in crowded clusters on the ground→species 7, *Clitocybe multiceps* (*Lyophyllum decastes*).

    b. Fruiting bodies growing singly or in troops on the ground, but not in dense clusters. Color and surface of cap vary→key 23.

23. a. Fruiting body very large, 8 to 16 inches in diameter, broadly funnel shaped; gills decurrent→genus *LEUCOPAXILLUS* (*CLITOCYBE*).

    A. Cap whitish to buff-tan, convex to flattened, becoming depressed and finally infundibuliform, mostly dry, smooth, slightly hairy at the margin. Gills slightly decurrent, whitish becoming dingy with age. Stem thick, short, stout, almost bulbous at the base, whitish like the cap→species 23, *Leucopaxillus* (*Clitocybe*) *giganteus*.

    b. Fruiting body seldom larger than 4 to 5 inches in diameter, not funnel-shaped; gills adnate and notched, not decurrent→genus *TRICHOLOMA*.

    A. Cap reddish brown to orange-red, viscid, becoming appressed-scaly, margin woolly, glutinous. Gills adnexed, close, whitish, becoming spotted and stained reddish brown. Stem more or less covered with rings of scales that are colored like the cap→species 37, *Tricholoma aurantium*.

    B. Cap pale to bright yellow, sometimes reddish or brownish at the center, viscid, smooth. Gills deeply notched appearing free, close, broad, sulphur yellow→species 38, *Tricholoma flavovirens*.

    C. Cap reddish brown, peel breaking into coarse imbricating scales. Gills adnate, whitish, becoming rufous with age. Stem pale reddish brown, solid, minutely striated and somewhat rooting→species 39, *Tricholoma imbricatum*.

D. Cap bright sulphur yellow, often with brown tinge at center, smooth and dry. Gills attached and toothed (notched), sulphur yellow. Stem fibrous, sulphur yellow and longitudinally striated. Odor unpleasant, of coal tar→species 40, *Tricholoma sulphureum*.

E. Cap mouse gray, dry, umbonate, fibrillose, becoming scaly to slightly woolly, scales dark gray to sooty. Gills adnexed, white to dingy white. Stem white, solid. Growing in clusters or troops on the ground→species 41, *Tricholoma terreum*.

24. a. Gills broadly adnate to decurrent. Fruiting body growing on the ground→genus *CLITOPILUS*.

    A. Cap white to ash gray, dry, feltlike or almost velvety, slightly viscid in damp air, covered with scurfy particles that fall off. Gills decurrent, separated, whitish becoming pale pink with age, interspaced with smaller gills. Stem dull white, upper surface with scurfy particles below the gills, base somewhat cottony→species 42, *Clitopilus prunulus*.

    b. Gills free. Fruiting body growing on wood→genus *PLUTEUS*.

    A. Cap dull dark brown to pale dingy fawn color, darkest at the center, sometimes streaked with darker fibrils. Gills free, broad, close, rounded near the stem, white, turning flesh pink or tan with age→species 43, *Pluteus cervinus*.

25. a. Gills attached. Annulus present or absent→key 26.
    b. Gills free. Annulus present, usually conspicuous→genus *AGARICUS*.

    A. Cap white with pale yellow patches, becoming light brown over all with age, campanulate then convex to flattened when fully expanded, with remains of a veil on the margin. Gills white at first, then pinkish gray, becoming tobacco brown with age. Stem whitish, becoming pale yellow to nut brown with age. Annulus a full double-skirted ring, outer layer membranous, inner layer woolly with a ragged margin, white to brownish, fragile→species 56, *Agaricus arvensis*.

    B. Cap white, becoming brownish when old, convex becoming flat, silky and shiny, margin extended and fringed with veil remnants. Gills bright pink becoming purple-brown and finally blackish with age. Stem white, silky above the ring, brownish below. Annulus thin, single white, fragile→species 57, *Agaricus campestris*.

C. Cap whitish beneath blackish brown fibrillose scales covering its surface. Gills white then grayish-purplish, eventually turning dark purple-brown. Stem whitish, staining yellowish, smooth. Annulus a large, conspicuous, double ring, whitish above, the lower layer cracking into brownish patches→species 58, *Agaricus meleagris (placomyces)*.

D. Cap white, dry, covered with densely arranged pinkish brown, somewhat hairy scales, turning reddish where bruised or cut. Gills whitish pink, becoming dark reddish brown or chocolate brown with age. Stem whitish, turning reddish where bruised, becoming dingy with age, having an enlarged, almost bulbous base. Annulus persistent, cottony beneath with raised buff patches, whitish becoming dingy→species 59, *Agaricus silvaticus*.

26. a. Cap and stem viscid; fruiting bodies growing singly, on the ground→genus *STROPHARIA*.

    A. Cap yellowish to brownish, slightly umbonate, viscid. Gills adnate, pale grayish becoming purplish brown. Stem viscid, yellow-brown. Annulus membranous, persistent→species 61, *Stropharia magnivelaris*.

    b. Neither cap nor stem viscid; fruiting bodies growing in clusters or dense troops on wood→genus *NAEMATOLOMA*.

    A. Cap bright reddish orange or yellow-brown, paler and more yellowish at the margin, smooth, slightly umbonate. Gills adnate, whitish then grayish, becoming purple-brown. Stem yellow above, rusty brown below, with a faint annular zone→species 60, *Naematoloma capnoides*.

27. a. Cortina (a loose, silky, cobwebby mass of threads) *lacking* on young specimens, annulus present or absent→key 29.
    b. Cortina present on young fruiting bodies→key 28.

28. a. Spores dull brown, gills dingy brown→genus *INOCYBE*, key 30b.
    b. Spores bright rusty brown, gills rusty brown→genus *CORTINARIUS*.

A. Cap yellow-brown, olive-brown, or cinnamon, dry. Gills adnate, close, yellow when young. Stem finely fibrillose, yellow or cinnamon-buff→species 44, *Cortinarius cinnamomeus*.

B. Cap often whitish when young, becoming yellowish to orange-yellow with age, very viscid when moist. Gills adnate with a tooth, pale violet, turning dull reddish brown with age. Stem covered with a pale violet, viscid universal veil, becoming stained rusty or yellowish toward the base—species 45, *Cortinarius collinitus*.

C. Cap tawny yellow to cinnamon-yellow, silky to minutely scaled. Gills adnate to decurrent, blood-red when young. Stem yellow to tawny→species 46, *Cortinarius semisanguineus*.

D. Cap pale lilac overall, dry, umbonate with age. Gills attached, lilac when young, becoming spore-stained yellowish brown with age. Stem club-shaped at base, dry, lilac above and below the fibrillose zone left by the collapsed cortina, flesh in the base of the stem rusty brown→species 47, *Cortinarius traganus*.

E. Cap dark violet, sometimes metallic-shiny, covered with small, erect tufts or scales, margin somewhat fringed. Gills adnate, dark violet. Stem dark violet on the outside, violaceous within→species 48, *Cortinarius violaceus*.

29. a. Annulus present→key 31.
    b. Annulus lacking→key 30.

30. a. Gills decurrent, yellow to olive-beige when young, quickly staining reddish brown where bruised; cap viscid when wet→genus *PAXILLUS*.

    A. Cap yellowish to reddish brown to olive brown with dark spots, smooth, convex, becoming flattened then depressed. Gills forked on the stem, olive-yellow, bruising brown. Stem same color as the cap or paler, often streaked with darker brown, sometimes excentric→species 51, *Paxillus involutus*.

    b. Gills not decurrent, white to pallid when young, not staining where bruised; cap not viscid when wet→genus *INOCYBE*.

    A. Cap cigar brown, fibrillose to somewhat scaly, sometimes olive-tinged at the faintly striate margin. Gills adnate, pale olive-gray. Stem rusty brown→species 50, *Inocybe lacera*.

31. a. Fruiting bodies growing on the ground, *and* cap, stem and annulus *not* covered with a granular-powdery substance→genus *ROZITES* (*PHOLIOTA*).

    A. Cap cinnamon-buff to ochraceous buff, paler at the margin, usually with a thin whitish bloom. Gills adnate, pallid, becoming brownish with age, sometimes marked with light and dark bands. Stem solid, whitish, smooth, sometimes scurfy with minute white scales at the top. Annulus large, membranous, remote (about the midpoint on the stem). Volva inconspicuous, delicate and filmy, whitish to yellowish, appearing as small thin patches on the base of stem→species 62, *Rozites* (*Pholiota*) *caperata*.

  b. Fruiting bodies growing on wood, or if terrestrial, then cap, stem and annulus covered with a granular-powdery substance→genus *PHOLIOTA*.

    A. Cap very large, golden brown, with a scurfy or granular coating that rubs off easily. Gills adnexed, rounded, clay color, becoming rusty yellow. Stem colored as the cap or paler, sheathed from below by a veil that breaks off at the margin of the cap leaving a membranous annulus. Annulus conspicuously large and pendulous, persistent, dark buff below, lemon yellow above→species 52, *Pholiota aurea*.

    B. Cap date brown when wet, fading to chamois or ginger color upon drying, frequently brick red in the center. Gills adnexed, close, interspaced with smaller gills, yellowish then cinnamon, finally rust colored. Stem colored like the cap, covered with dark reddish brown scales below the annulus, becoming hollow with age→species 53, *Pholiota* (*Kuehneromyces*) *mutabilis*.

    C. Cap saffron yellow to tan, covered with stiff, upturned brownish scales, dry. Gills pale yellow, becoming rusty red. Stem colored like the cap, and covered with brownish scales. Annulus conspicuous, paler than the cap or stem→species 54, *Pholiota squarrosa*.

    D. Cap golden brown over all, viscid, with glutinous, brownish, triangular scales. Gills straw yellow, turning rusty red. Stem yellow, smooth above, scaly below. Annulus thin, incomplete, or lacking→ species 54, *Pholiota squarroso-adiposa*.

32. a. Cap and lower stem viscid; gills decurrent, not dissolving into a black, inky fluid→genus *GOMPHIDIUS*.

A. Cap livid purple-brown, smooth, viscid to glutinous, often having the remains of a viscid veil. Gills decurrent, forked, waxy, whitish at first, becoming smoky gray to blackish. Stem whitish to pale brownish, yellow at the base, sheathed by a viscid veil that leaves an annular line near the top→species 66, *Gomphidius glutinosus*.

b. Cap and stem not viscid; gills not decurrent, dissolving into a black, inky fluid→genus *COPRINUS*.

A. Cap gray to brownish, lobed and folded, silky smooth, conic to campanulate, becoming tattered on the margin with age. Gills white, becoming black and dissolving into an inky fluid→species 63, *Coprinus atramentarius*.

B. Cap cylindrical or barrel-shaped, gradually expanding and becoming somewhat "bell-shaped," covered with shaggy brownish scales exposing the white flesh beneath. Gills white, turning pink then black and gradually dissolving into an inky fluid, starting at the margin of the cap and going upward→species 64, *Coprinus comatus*.

C. Cap tan to ochraceous brown, fading to whitish with age and covered with minute glistening particles, strongly striated. Gills whitish, turning purplish to black and dissolving into an inky fluid→species 65, *Coprinus micaceus*.

KEYS TO THE MUSHROOMS WITHOUT GILLS

FLESHY PORE FUNGI, FAMILY *BOLETACEAE*

33. a. Stem hollow, with an annulus (may be delicate, and sometimes adheres to the margin of the cap); pores (tubes) noticeably radially elongated→genus *SUILLUS* (*BOLETINUS*), one species: species 73, *Suillus* (*Boletinus*) *cavipes*.
    b. Stem solid, lacking an annulus; pores not radially elongated→key 34.

34. a. Flesh, tubes, and pores white to pale ivory, becoming lemon yellow with age→genus *CALOPORUS* (*POLYPORUS*), in family *Polyporaceae*, key 40b.
    b. Flesh, pores, and tubes not all white or pale ivory, and becoming lemon yellow with age→key 35.

35. a. Stem covered with small, blackish, rather stiff projections, conspicuous against a pale or white ground color→genus *LECCINUM*, key 36.
b. Stem not covered with small, dotlike, blackish projections→genus *BOLETUS*, key 38.

36. a. Cap grayish brown, without red or orange tones; flesh of cap not becoming gray where cut or bruised→species 71, *Leccinum scabrum*.
b. Cap red-brown, reddish, or orange; flesh of cap becoming first purplish or reddish then gray to blackish where cut or bruised→key 37.

37. a. Flesh of cap where exposed slowly staining reddish purplish, then gray. Flesh of stem often becoming blue at the base where cut. Ornamentation of the stem whitish in young specimens→species 70, *Leccinum aurantiacum*.
b. Flesh of cap staining reddish (not purplish) then gray. Flesh of stem not becoming blue in the base where cut. Ornamentation of the stem black from the first→species 72, *Leccinum insigne*.

38. a. All parts of the fruiting body staining blue where cut or bruised→species 68, *Boletus erythropus*.
b. No part of the fruiting body staining blue where cut or bruised→key 39.

39. a. Cap and stem red-brown or bay, cap covered with tiny plushy, wartlike scales. Fruiting bodies growing on or alongside of rotting conifer wood→species 69, *Boletus mirabilis*.
b. Cap clay-colored or crust-brown, smooth; stem pallid or pale brown, sometimes tinged cinnamon in the middle. Fruiting bodies not growing on or alongside rotting conifer wood→species 67, *Boletus edulis*.

WOODY PORE FUNGI, FAMILY *POLYPORACEAE*

40. a. Fruiting bodies always growing on wood, or if from the ground, then from buried wood, such as roots. Not mushroomlike with cap and stem. Not white becoming lemon yellow with age→key 41.
b. Fruiting bodies growing on the ground, not attached to wood. Mushroomlike with cap and stem. Flesh, tubes and pores whitish, becoming lemon yellow with age→genus *CALOPORUS (POLYPORUS)*, one species: species 74, *Caloporus (Polyporus) ovinus (Albatrellus ovinus, Scutiger ovinus)*.

41. a. Fruiting bodies forming massive clusters colored bright sulphur yellow to orange; mostly on spruce or cottonwood, occasionally on other woods→genus *LAETIPORUS (POLYPORUS)*, one species: species 75, *Laetiporus (Polyporus) sulphureus.*
b. Fruiting bodies growing singly or in clusters, but not bright lemon yellow to orange→key 42.

42. a. Fruiting bodies growing singly, circular to oval in outline as seen from above, with thick, inrolled sterile margin projecting below the pore surface, attached by a lateral stemlike knob (umbo); growing on birch→genus *POLYPORUS,* species 76, *Polyporus (Piptoporus) betulinus.*
b. Fruiting bodies growing in small to extensive clusters of overlapping shelves, colorfully zoned, with velvety or hairy surface; growing on hardwood, seldom on conifers→genus *POLYPORUS,* species 77, *Polyporus (Polystictus) versicolor.*

TOOTHED, OR HEDGEHOG, FUNGI, FAMILY *HYDNACEAE*

43. a. Fruiting body a mass of white or pallid fleshy branches bearing downward-pointing soft spines, not at all mushroomlike; growing on wood→genus *HERICIUM,* one species: species 79, *Hericium laciniatum.*
b. Fruiting bodies mushroomlike with cap and stem; growing on the ground→key 44.

44. a. Spore color white in a spore print→genus *DENTINUM (HYDNUM),* one species: species 78, *Dentinum (Hydnum) repandum.*
b. Spore color brown in a spore print→genus *HYDNUM,* key 45.

45. a. Flesh bitter. Flesh of base of stem dull blue-green to almost black, at least at the surface. Spines brown with whitish tips→species 81, *Hydnum fennicum.*
b. Flesh mild tasting. Flesh of base of stem not blue-green to almost black. Spines buff to grayish or bluish gray→species 80, *Hydnum imbricatum.*

CLUB, OR CORAL, FUNGI, FAMILY *CLAVARIACEAE*

46. a. Fruiting bodies not (or rarely and very sparsely) branched, but club-shaped or shaped like a spatula→key 47.

b. Fruiting bodies much branched, corallike, usually large, fleshy, fragile→key 50.

47. a. Fruiting body with the upper portion flattened and shaped like a short, blunt spatula→genus *SPATHULARIA,* family *GEOGLOSSACEAE,* key 62.
b. Fruiting body club-shaped or spindle-shaped or like a narrow trumpet, not flattened and spatulalike→genus *CLAVARIADELPHUS,* key 48.

48. a. Fruiting body shaped like a narrow trumpet, with flared, flattened or concave tip 1-1/2 to 2-1/2 inches broad, large, up to 3-1/2 to 6 inches tall→species 88, *Clavariadelphus truncatus.*
b. Fruiting body smaller than the above, club-shaped or spindle-shaped, with the tip rounded or sometimes inflated but not flat or concave→key 49.

49. a. Spores ocher or buff in a spore print→species 87, *Clavariadelphus sachaliensis.*
b. Spores white in a spore print→species 86, *Clavariadelphus pistillaris.*

50. a. Fruiting bodies growing on wood. Tips of all branches cup-shaped, with small, fingerlike projections growing from the rim of the cup. Taste peppery→species 85, *Clavicorona (Clavaria) pyxidata.*
b. Fruiting bodies growing on the ground. Tips of the branches rounded to toothed, but not cup-shaped. Taste mild→key 51.

51. a. Spores white to yellowish buff in a spore print. Fruiting bodies white to gray or tinged lavender→species 84, *Clavaria cristata.*
b. Spores buff, ocher, or dull yellow in a spore print. Fruiting bodies pink, violet, or yellow→genus *RAMARIA,* key 52.

52. a. Fruiting body pink to violet, sometimes lavender; resembles a cauliflower in appearance→species 82, *Ramaria (Clavaria) rufescens.*
b. Fruiting body bright yellow, with many branches arising from a short, thick, whitish base→species 83, *Ramaria (Clavaria) flava.*

SAC, OR SPONGE, FUNGI, FAMILY *HELVELLACEAE*

53. a. Cap folded, convoluted (brainlike), wrinkled, or smooth, but not pitted→key 54.
b. Cap oval to cone-shaped, covered with honeycomblike pits→key 57.

54. a. Cap bell-shaped or like a thimble, attached to the stem only at the apex and hanging down around it; margin free from the stem; surface prominently ridged, with network of veins→genus *VERPA,* one species: species 94, *Verpa bohemica.*
   b. Cap not bell-shaped or thimblelike→key 55.

55. a. Cap gray or black or occasionally white; irregularly folded and lobed, appearing crumpled. Stem deeply grooved, pitted, and ridged, same color as the cap or paler→genus *HELVELLA,* one species: species 91, *Helvella lacunosa.*
   b. Cap brown. Stem brown or pallid, not pitted or ridged→genus *GYROMITRA (HELVELLA)* key 56.

56. a. Cap more or less lobed, very irregular in shape, the surface brainlike in appearance, wrinkled and folded or convoluted→species 89, *Gyromitra (Helvella) esculenta.*
   b. Cap somewhat saddle-shaped, rising to a peak on either side of the stem, with a saddlelike depression between them, the surface smooth to undulating or shallowly convoluted or folded→species 90, *Helvella infula.*

57. a. Cap elongated to conic, hollow, with grooved attachment by its margin to the top of the stem; surface covered with long pits in vertical rows→species 92, *Morchella angusticeps.*
   b. Cap oval to almost globose; surface covered with pits of various shapes and in no orderly arrangement→species 93, *Morchella esculenta.*

PUFFBALLS, OR STOMACH FUNGI, FAMILY *LYCOPERDACEAE*

58. a. Small, inverted pear-shaped puffballs. Base attached by a fiberlike, mycelial, rootlike strand, and often prolonged into a short, stout, stemlike base. Top of fruiting body with a pore through which the spores escape→genus *LYCOPERDON,* key 59.
   b. Large, globose puffballs with a thick, cordlike, rooting mycelium. Outer covering thin and smooth or somewhat scaly. Lacking a pore; the spores liberated by the splitting and falling away of the outer covering→genus *CALVATIA,* one species: species 95, *Calvatia gigantea.*

59. a. Outer covering whitish and densely covered with fragile spines surrounded by small warts. Growing in clumps and clusters on the ground→species 96, *Lycoperdon perlatum.*
   b. Outer covering yellowish or brownish yellow, covered with smaller,

darker brown, rather harsh-feeling warts. Growing on rotting stumps and logs, often in large clusters→species 97, *Lycoperdon pyriforme.*

CUP FUNGI, FAMILY *PEZIZACEAE*

60. a. Cups some shade of brown, inside and out, or at least in the lining of the cup→genus *PEZIZA,* key 61.
b. Inner surface of cup bright orange or reddish orange, outer surface paler orange when wet, dingy white when dry→genus *ALEURIA,* one species: species 100, *Aleuria (Peziza) aurantia.*

61. a. Cups red-brown to brown inside and out. Growing on the ground→species 98, *Peziza badio-confusa.*
b. Cups pale brown inside, whitish outside, becoming expanded and flattened. Growing on rotted logs and buried wood→species 99, *Peziza repanda.*

EARTH TONGUES, FAMILY *GEOGLOSSACEAE*

62. Fruiting body with round stem and flattened, spatula-shaped top, yellow or buff. Growing on the ground among moss and needles→genus *SPATHULARIA,* one species: species 101, *Spathularia flavida (clavata).*

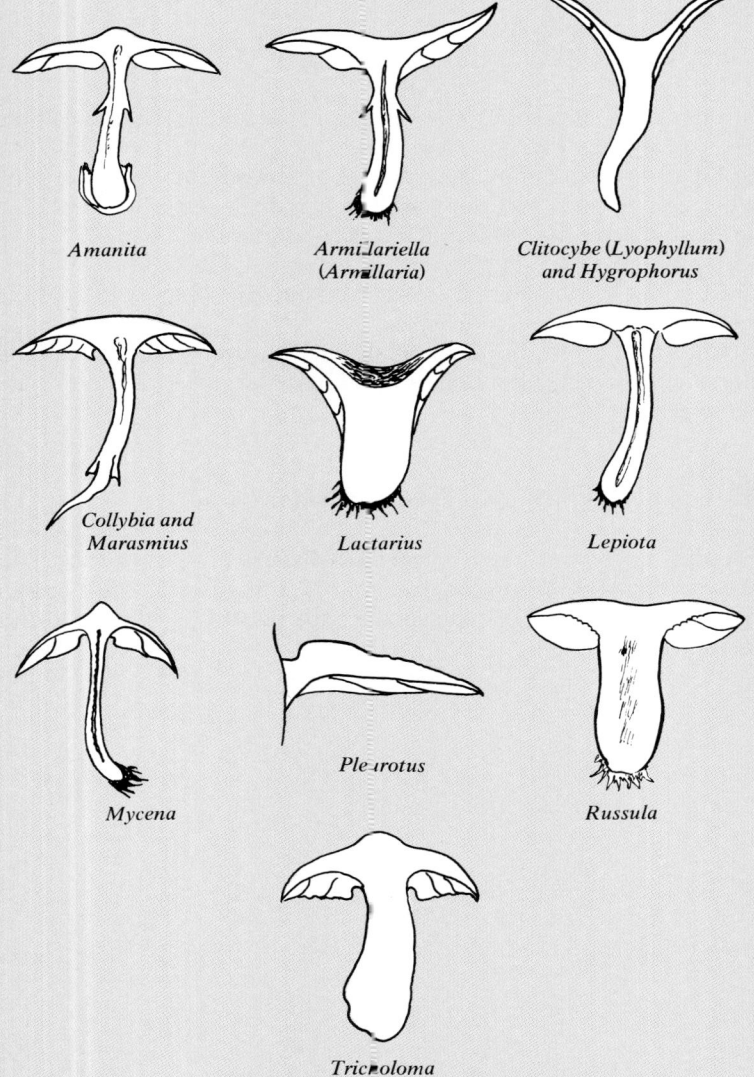

Figure 5—Gilled Mushrooms—Family *Agaricaceae*—With Spores Colorless, White, Cream, Yellow or Buff

Chapter 5
Gilled Mushrooms Part One

Family Agaricaceae With Spores Colorless, White, Cream, Yellow or Buff

This chapter includes descriptions of 41 species of the family *Agaricaceae* (color plate numbers 1 through 41) representing the following 18 genera:

Amanita	*Flammulina (Collybia)*	*Limacella*
Armillariella (Armillaria)	*Hygrophorus*	*Marasmius*
Cantharellus	*Laccaria*	*Mycena*
Catathelasma	*Lactarius*	*Pleurotus*
Clitocybe (Lyophyllum)	*Lepiota*	*Russula*
Collybia	*Leucopaxillus (Clitocybe)*	*Tricholoma*

Cross sections of typical mushrooms are shown in Figure 5.

To be sure of identifying mushrooms correctly, use the keys given in Chapter 4.

GENUS AMANITA

This genus is distinguished by the combination of at least three principal characters: 1) white spore color, 2) a volva or cup at the base of the stem, and 3) a persistent cottony annulus or ring on the stem. Other important characteristics are: whitish gills that are typically free from the stem, and a stem that readily separates from the cap. Great care must be taken in collecting these and similar gilled mushrooms so that all of the mushroom is gotten out of the ground. The distinctive volva is sometimes left when the mushroom is cut or pulled, and one may be fooled into thinking it was not present.

The amanitas are the most deadly of all the known mushrooms in the world, so any collector should become very familiar with the species to be found in his particular area. Some amanitas are considered to be edible, but I would not chance eating any mushrooms of this group, or any closely resembling them. There are sufficient others to fill the need for food.

Gilled—Spores White to Buff

The button stage of the amanitas is similar in appearance to some puffballs (edible), but the similarity is soon lost at cutting through an amanita and a puffball and comparing them (see Figures 3, 5 and 12, on pages 5, 32 and 171). The button amanita will show evidence of a cap, gills and stem structures, while the puffball will be homogeneously white throughout, showing none of these structures.

1. Amanita muscaria
Fly agaric; poisonous. Spores white. ─────────────

Cap—3 to 8 inches wide. Rounded, becoming flattened to convex, viscid when fresh; color varies from red to scarlet, orange, yellow fading to whitish in exposed areas, covered with thick whitish to buff floccose warts.
Gills—Free, sometimes reaching the stem, close together, almost crowded, broad; white to cream color, often slightly woolly on the edges.
Flesh—White to creamy, thick at the center of the cap, thinning to a line at the margin, tinged pale yellow under the cuticle (peel).
Stem—4 to 8 inches long, 1/2 to 3/4 inch thick. Mostly equal but sometimes tapering slightly upward above the volva, stuffed, whitish to yellow color, smooth above, scaly lower down from the remains of the torn volva.
Annulus—Large, membranous, white to yellowish, persistent.
Volva—Whitish to buff or straw color; broken into shaggy rings or scales on the bulbous base of the stem and appears as thick warts on the young cap.
Odor—Not distinctive.
Taste—Not distinctive. Never taste any amanita.
Habitat—On the ground, solitary or in scattered groups or in large colonies, sometimes in rings, along roadsides, open woods and fields from July to October.
Notes—The most poisonous mushroom in Alaska. It is especially dangerous to children who are attracted by its bright color. The principal poison is ibotenic acid-muscimol; other symptoms are caused by the secondary poison muscarine. Symptoms will usually appear within an hour after the mushroom has been eaten. There is a brief period of drowsiness, and a state of excitement resembling alcoholic intoxication characterized by confusion, muscle spasms, delirium, hallucinations and vision disturbances. This state may last for 4 hours or more, or until the victim falls into a deep comalike sleep. Death seldom results to healthy adults, and recovery is usually within 24 hours.

Amanita muscaria

2. Amanita porphyria
Purple-brown amanita; poisonous. Spores white.

Cap—Usually 1 to 2-1/2 inches, sometimes 4 to 5 inches wide, becoming flattened, convex, occasionally subumbonate. Grayish brown with slight purplish tinge. Smooth, viscid, usually having a few remnants of the crumbling volva on the decurved nonstriated margin.
Gills—Free, close, moderately broad, creamy white color.
Flesh—Thin, whitish.
Stem—2 to 4-1/2 inches long, 1/4 to 1/2 inch thick. Equal or tapering slightly upward above the soft rounded bulb, often gray-flecked on a white background.
Annulus—Thin, membranous, ashy gray color, collapsing against the stem.
Volva—Pallid or grayish on the bulb, usually separates at the margin of the cap, leaving gray patches, and at the base of the stem.
Odor—Not distinctive.
Taste—Not distinctive. Never taste any amanita.
Habitat—Solitary or in groups of several, on the ground in open woods from August to October.
Notes—There is some evidence that *A. porphyria* is as poisonous as *A. muscaria*. You should not chance to eat any of the amanita species. Refer to Chapter 3, MUSHROOM POISONS, for information on the amanita.

Amanita porphyria

3. Amanita (Amanitopsis) vaginata
Sheathed amanitopsis, grisette; edible, but dangerous. Spores white.

Cap—2 to 4 inches wide. Soft, at first ovate, becoming campanulate or convex, then flattened, umbonate. Surface smooth or occasionally having remnants of the volva. Margin grooved, striated. There appear to be three color forms or variants to the caps: 1) whitish, 2) tawny or brownish (the most common in Southcentral Alaska) and 3) grayish.
Gills—Free, not close, moderately broad, whitish in color.
Flesh—Moderately thin, white.
Stem—3 to 7 inches long, about 1/4 inch thick tapering slightly upward. Base not bulbous, extending some distance into the ground, stuffed, becoming hollow, surface smooth, somewhat mealy or granular, whitish color.
Annulus—None.
Volva—Large, white, membranous, mostly underground, encasing the base of the stem and collapsing against it.
Odor—Not distinctive.
Taste—Not distinctive. Never taste any amanita.
Habitat—Solitary or scattered on the ground in open woods and on slopes of mountains from July to October.
Notes—This mushroom is considered edible, but dangerous because a poisonous amanita species could be mistaken for it. Never chance eating any of the amanitas.

Amanita (Amanitopsis) vaginata 39

GENUS ARMILLARIELLA (ARMILLARIA)

This genus is characterized by having white spores, gills that are attached to the stem and an annulus on the stem that may disappear with age. There is no volva at the stem base. *Armillariella (Armillaria) mellea* is typical of the genus and very common in Alaska. It is almost always found growing on wood, seldom on the ground unless growing from an underground root.

4. Armillariella (Armillaria) mellea
Honey mushroom; edible. Spores white.

Cap—1-1/4 to 4 inches wide. Acorn-shaped to round at first with inrolled margin, then flattened or convex; sometimes subumbonate. Color varies from yellow-buff, yellow-brown or rusty-tinged; minutely scaled with buff to brown or blackish tufts of fibrils, becoming striate on the margin.
Gills—Adnate or subdecurrent, close to subdistant, moderately broad, at first white to creamy, staining rusty brown.
Flesh—Thin, slightly thicker on the disk, whitish to rusty-tinged.
Stem—2 to 6 inches long, 1/4 to 3/4 inch thick. About equal or broadening below to a clavate base, stuffed then hollow, finely fibrillose to scaly, paler color than the cap, especially at its apex, becoming rusty-stained with age.
Annulus—White or tinged brownish. Fibrillose-membranous, subpersistent to disappearing with age.
Volva—None.
Odor—Mild to slightly unpleasant.
Taste—Mild to slightly acrid and unpleasant.
Habitat—In dense clusters around the base of living trees and old stumps from July to October.
Notes—Select only the young specimens for food; old specimens are likely to be strong tasting and very tough.

Armillariella (Armillaria) mellea

GENUS CANTHARELLUS

This genus is characterized by having a white spore color, usually narrow, brightly colored funnel-form caps with decurrent gills having thick edges, ridgelike in appearance. The stems are usually central and colored as the caps. These may be confused with species of *Clitocybe* and *Hygrophorus,* but once recognized are easily known. They grow singly or in groups on the ground in mixed woods.

5. Cantharellus tubaeformis
Tubelike chantarelle; edible with caution. Spores yellowish white.____

Cap—3/4 to 2 inches wide. At first convex, becoming depressed, slightly infundibuliform; may become perforated at the center with age. Brownish yellow to ochraceous. Slightly silky-hairy, margin irregular and wavy.
Gills—Decurrent, distant, narrow, blunt on the edge and forming a ridge, forked, at first yellowish, becoming grayish with age.
Flesh—Thin, whitish ochraceous.
Stem—1 to 2-1/2 inches long, 1/8 to 1/4 inch thick, equal, smooth, brownish yellow to ochraceous, whitish at the base, solid, sometimes becoming hollow with age.
Annulus—None.
Volva—None.
Odor—None.
Taste—None.
Habitat—In groups on the ground in swampy places, usually among sphagnum, from July to September.
Notes—*C. tubaeformis* is closely allied with other chantarelles that have caused mild poisoning in some people. It is best to try a small piece at first and wait several hours before eating a larger quantity of this mushroom.

Cantharellus tubaeformis

GENUS CATATHELASMA

This genus includes some very large robust mushrooms with decurrent gills and a double annulus (ring) on the stem. The spore color is white. Mostly found growing singly on the ground in mixed woods, sometimes in groups.

6. Catathelasma imperialis
Edible but may be unpalatable. Spores colorless.

Cap—3 to 8 inches, sometimes to 18 inches. Very firm, at first rounded, becoming flattened. The buttons may be as large as baseballs. Whitish to smoky gray color with darker fibrils near the margin. Smooth, slightly viscid, sometimes becoming cracked, margin decurved, strongly inrolled at first.
Gills—Decurrent, white to yellowish, close, moderately narrow, sometimes forked.
Flesh—White, very thick, firm.
Stem—2 to 5 inches long, 1/2 to 1 inch thick. Narrowing to a point at its base. Color very similar to the color of the cap, sometimes a bit more yellowish. Scaly, solid.
Annulus—Double, the outer ring membranous and colored like the cap, the inner ring more filamentous, whitish, may soon disappear.
Volva—None.
Odor—None.
Taste—Strong; may be unpleasant.
Habitat—Singly or in groups on the ground under conifers in August and September.
Notes—This mushroom is easily found in season, and a very few buttons make a large meal. Unfortunately, the flavor is not particularly good, and the stems are inclined to be a bit tough when cooked.

GENUS CLITOCYBE (LYOPHYLLUM)

The species of this genus are mostly white-spored, and have gills that are decurrent on the stem. They lack both volva and annulus. The stem is fibrous, similar to the cap in texture and not easily separated from it. *Clitocybe* is a large genus and many of the small whitish species are difficult to identify. Most appear to be edible, but information is lacking on several, and at least two, *Clitocybe illudens* and *Clitocybe dealbata,* are known to be poisonous.

7. Clitocybe multiceps (Lyophyllum decastes)
Fried chicken mushroom; edible. Spores white._____

Cap—1 to 3 inches or wider. Convex, often irregular in outline when clustered. Whitish, often tinged with buff or gray. Moist, smooth. Thin margin, often wavy.
Gills—Adnate to slightly decurrent or sinuate, close, moderately broad in center, narrowing at each end, whitish color.
Flesh—White, thick on the disk, thin at the margin.
Stem—2 to 5 inches long, 1/4 to 1/2 inch thick. Moderately stout, subequal to tapering slightly upward. Smooth to slightly scaly. Whitish. Solid, mostly central, but slightly excentric in clusters.
Annulus—None.
Volva—None.
Odor—None.
Taste—None.
Habitat—In clusters, often crowded, on the ground in grassy places and open woods from July to October.
Notes—Very common in Alaska and, properly prepared, a delight to eat. Tastes like fried chicken when rolled in a batter and deep fried. Caution: Do not confuse it with the poisonous *Entoloma lividum,* which looks much like *C. multiceps* before the gills of *E. lividum* become pink.

Clitocybe multiceps (Lyophyllum decastes)

GENUS COLLYBIA

This genus contains many small species that are of little value as food. The spore color is white. Gills are adnate to adnexed on cartilaginous stems. The margin of the cap is inrolled at first becoming elevated with age. The mushrooms lack both a volva and an annulus. No poisonous species of *Collybia* are known, but *Collybia dryophila* may be inedible for some people. Some of the larger species are gathered for food and are said to have a good flavor.

8. Collybia acervata
Edible. Spores white. _____

Cap—3/4 to 2 inches wide. Flattened, smooth, watery. Reddish to vinaceous brown, margin paler and fading to nearly whitish. Striate when moist, sometimes wavy and irregular, upturned when mature.
Gills—Free to adnexed, crowded, narrow, tinged whitish to reddish.
Flesh—Thin, pallid.
Stem—2 to 4 inches or longer 1/8 to 1/4 inch thick. Equal, hollow; smooth above; whitish-hairy below. Densely tufted and often bound together. Reddish to vinaceous brown, often darker than the cap.
Annulus—None.
Volva—None.
Odor—Not distinctive.
Taste—Mild; slightly bitter when old.
Habitat—In dense clusters or tufts on the ground or on rotten wood from August to October.
Notes—A small species and of not much value as food. Taste is reported to be bitterish even after cooking.

Collybia acervata 49

9. Collybia dryophila
Inedible to some people; dangerous. Spores white.

Cap—1 to 2 inches wide. Thin, flattened, irregular and wavy. Surface smooth, moist when fresh. Color varies from yellowish to reddish tan, fading with age.
Gills—Adnate to adnexed, narrow, crowded, whitish to pallid.
Flesh—Thin, whitish.
Stem—1-1/4 to 2-1/2 inches long. 1/8 inch thick. Cartilaginous. Equal or tapering upward; often compound; central or slightly excentric. Hollow, smooth, colored like the cap, often tufted at the base.
Annulus—None.
Volva—None.
Odor—Not distinctive.
Taste—Not distinctive.
Habitat—In clusters or groups on the ground in woods. Commonly found from late June through September.
Notes—There are several closely related collybias that might be mistaken for *C. dryophila*. This mushroom is said to disagree with some people, so caution should be exercised However, it is a very small species and not of much value as food.

GENUS FLAMMULINA (COLLYBIA)

10. Flammulina (Collybia) velutipes
Velvet-stemmed mushroom; edible. Spores white. ─────────

Cap—3/4 to 2 inches wide. Flattened, often irregular. Surface smooth, viscid, outer layer easily removed. Color varies from yellowish to reddish to brown.
Gills—Sinuate-adnexed, broad, subdistant, yellowish, edges slightly fringed.
Flesh—Moderately thick, white or tinged yellowish to reddish.
Stem—3/4 to 2-1/2 inches long, 1/8 to 1/4 inch thick, tough. Equal or tapering slightly downward toward the base. Stuffed to hollow when old, surface densely velvety-hairy. Bright cinnamon color, usually yellowish upper, dark brown or blackish toward the base. Most always in clusters.
Annulus—None.
Volva—None.
Odor—Not distinctive.
Taste—Mild.
Habitat—In clusters mostly, but may occur singly on decaying logs and stumps, sometimes on the bark of living trees.
Notes—Found chiefly in late autumn (October), but sometimes found in the spring and summer depending on the conditions for growth. Hardy in cold weather and may appear during mild spells in January and February. It is best to remove the tough outer layer before cooking.

Flammulina (Collybia) velutipes 53

GENUS HYGROPHORUS

This white-spored genus is characterized by gills that are adnexed to decurrent on the stem, usually thick and more or less triangular in cross section, moderately distant with a waxy texture. It is a large genus that includes some very colorful mushrooms and several good edible species. Only one, *Hygrophorus conicus* might be considered as inedible to some people, but it is easily recognized by its orange to red-orange conical cap and by flesh that blackens when bruised.

11. Hygrophorus conicus
Cone-shaped waxy cap; edible to most people. Spores white._____

Cap—1 to 2 inches wide. Conic and remains so. Orange, red-orange or yellowish; tinged with olive to blackish streaks; blackening when bruised or in age. Smooth, viscid when wet, becoming dry. Margin often splits as the cap expands; sometimes lobed.
Gills—Almost free, moderately close and broad, especially in the center. Pallid yellowish color.
Flesh—Thin, tinged orange.
Stem—1-1/2 to 3-1/2 inches long, 1/8 to 1/4 inch thick, equal. Yellowish or orange-tinged, blackening where bruised. Becoming hollow, striated, twisting, readily splitting lengthwise.
Annulus—None.
Volva—None.
Odor—Not distinctive.
Taste—Not distinctive.
Habitat—Singly or in groups, never in a cluster, on the ground in open woods and fields from July to October.
Notes—Some investigators list *H. conicus* as a suspect, others say it is nonpoisonous or edible with caution. It is a small mushroom and that, along with its ability to turn blackish when bruised, makes it undesirable to some people.

Hygrophorus conicus 55

12. Hygrophorus chrysodon
Edible. Spores white. _____

Cap—1 to 3 inches wide. Convex with margin incurved, becoming flattened, sometimes slightly umbonate. White, viscid when fresh, sprinkled with yellow granules.
Gills—Decurrent, broad, slightly distant, white.
Flesh—Soft, white, thick at the disk, thinner at the margin.
Stem—1-1/2 to 4 inches long, 1/4 to 1/2 inch thick. Equal or tapering downward, stuffed, viscid when fresh. Whitish, sprinkled with yellow granules, especially at the top where they may form a yellowish annular zone.
Annulus—None.
Volva—None.
Odor—Mild.
Taste—Mild.
Habitat—Mostly in groups on the ground in open woods from September to October.
Notes—Some investigators list *H. chrysodon* as an unknown, but most list it as an edible mushroom.

Hygrophorus chrysodon

13. Hygrophorus eburneus
Edible. Spores white.———————————————————————

Cap—1 to 3 inches wide. Glutinous, convex to flattened, subumbonate. White. Margin slightly woolly and incurved becoming expanded and elevated with age.
Gills—Decurrent-subdecurrent, distant, moderately broad, narrowing toward the margin. White, becoming dingy with age.
Flesh—White, thick.
Stem—2 to 6 inches long, 1/8 to 3/8 inch thick. Subequal or tapering downward, stuffed becoming hollow with age, glutinous. White, becoming dingy with age, top of stem dotted with small scales.
Annulus—None.
Volva—None.
Odor—Not distinctive.
Taste—Not distinctive.
Habitat—Mostly in groups on the ground in open woods from September and October.
Notes—The very glutinous cap and stem distinguishes this mushroom easily. It is somewhat shiny when dry. Some collectors shy away from eating *H. eburneus* because of the slimy coating, which should be removed before cooking.

Hygrophorus eburneus

GENUS LACCARIA

The mushrooms of this genus are somewhat small with white or pale lilac spore color. They all have thickish, somewhat waxy-looking, gills that are purplish to flesh-colored. All species lack an annulus or volva. The *Laccaria* species are likely to be confused with *Hygrophorus* or *Lactarius* species that have dried up. All the *Laccaria* species are reputed to be edible, but not very good in flavor.

14. Laccaria laccata
Edible. Spores white. _____

Cap—3/4 to 2 inches, sometimes 3 inches, wide. Convex, becoming flattened, slightly umbilicate, smooth at first then somewhat scaly, hygrophanous. Color varies from reddish brown to reddish flesh color or pallid. Margin even or wavy and notched.
Gills—Emarginate to decurrent, broad, moderately distant, thick, tinged flesh color.
Flesh—Thin, moist.
Stem—1 to 4 inches long, 1/8 to 3/8 inch thick. Equal, tough, fibrous, smooth to scaly, sometimes striate; stuffed, becoming hollow with age. Same color as the cap.
Annulus—None.
Volva—None.
Odor—Not distinctive.
Taste—Mild.
Habitat—Singly or in large groups on the ground in open woods as early as late May, mostly June to October.
Notes—One of the most common mushrooms in Alaska.

Laccaria laccata 61

GENUS LACTARIUS

This genus of mushrooms is distinguished by the presence of a latex or milky juice of various colors in young specimens. The spore color is mostly white or whitish. Color and taste of the latex are important characteristics in identifying the species, as well as the color changes when the latex is exposed to the air. Color of the cap and gills is also important for identification. Usually confused with the genus *Russula,* they are readily distinguished by the latex, of which *Russula* has none. *Lactarius deliciosus* is an excellent species for the table, but because certain other species of *Lactarius* are considered poisoncus, or at least sickeners, care should be exercised when collecting them for food.

15. Lactarius controversus
Controversial milky cap; inedible. Spores white.———————————

Cap—3 to 8 inches wide. Umbilicate, becoming depressed then infundibuliform. Whitish to flesh-colored, stained with brownish to flesh-colored spots. Slightly zoned toward the margin. Viscid, slightly hairy. Margin at first inrolled and then elevated with age.
Gills—Slightly decurrent, narrow, crowded, whitish to pink color.
Flesh—Firm, white to flesh color. Latex white.
Stem—1 to 1-1/2 inches long, 1/4 to 1 inch thick. Equal or tapering toward the base, slightly woolly, white or slightly stained, solid, frequently excentric.
Annulus—None.
Volva—None.
Odor—Not distinctive.
Taste—Becoming slowly acrid.
Habitat—Solitary or in groups on the ground. Associated with cottonwood, poplar and aspen in moist woods from August to October.
Notes—A large species. The flesh-colored cap and pinkish gills are distinctive, but the spots on the cap are sometimes not very conspicuous. The acrid latex makes this mushroom inedible.

Lactarius controversus 63

16. Lactarius deliciosus
Orange delight, orange milky cap; edible. Spores pale cream.⸺

Cap—2 to 5 inches wide. Fleshy and firm, convex, umbilicate early, then flattened with a depressed center. Reddish orange color, often with brighter concentric zones, facing to grayish or gray-green. Smooth, viscid when moist, margin at first inrolled, then arched and spreading.
Gills—Adnate-decurrent, close, rather narrow; orange, becoming greenish when bruised.
Flesh—Whitish, stained orange when broken, becoming greenish. Latex orange or reddish orange.
Stem—1-1/2 to 4 inches long, 1/2 to 3/4 inch thick. Equal or slightly narrowed at the base, smooth, same color as the cap or paler, sometimes with orange spots, becoming hollow in age.
Annulus—None.
Volva—None.
Odor—Not distinctive.
Taste—Mild.
Habitat—Singly or in groups scattered on the ground in moist boggy places of conifer woods from July to October.
Notes—An important edible mushroom easily recognized by the orange latex and the color of the cap. It has a good flavor and can usually be found in abundance in season.

Lactarius deliciosus

17. Lactarius mucidus
Slimy milky cap; inedible. Spores white. ─────────────

Cap—1 to 3 inches wide, convex, umbilicate, becoming flattened and depressed to infundibuliform. Grayish, putty-colored at the margin to brownish at the center. Viscid, smooth, not zoned, margin at first inrolled, then spreading.
Gills—Adnate, close to subdistant, narrow, some forked, white, staining greenish gray, sometimes staining bluish when bruised.
Flesh—Whitish, thin. Latex white, drying greenish to bluish gray.
Stem—1 to 2 inches long, 1/4 to 3/8 inch thick. Equal or tapering upward, viscid, smooth, somewhat wrinkled, same color as the cap or paler, becoming hollow with age.
Annulus—None.
Volva—None.
Odor—Not distinctive.
Taste—Acrid.
Habitat—Singly or in groups on the ground in conifer woods from July to October.
Notes—Commonly found with other *Lactarius* species. The acrid latex makes this mushroom inedible.

Lactarius mucidus

18. Lactarius representaneus
Inedible. Spores white._____

Cap—3 to 6 inches wide. Convex, becoming flattened. Dull yellow. Viscid, hairy, not zoned, margin at first inrolled and very hairy/woolly.
Gills—Adnate to slightly decurrent, close, moderately broad, dull yellowish, staining lilac when bruised. Latex white, becoming lilac-colored.
Flesh—Firm, whitish, becoming lilac-colored.
Stem—2 to 2-1/2 inches long, 3/4 to 1-1/4 inches thick. Equal, smooth, covered with a bloom at the top, hairy at the base, yellowish color with brighter spots, hollow.
Annulus—None.
Volva—None.
Odor—Not distinctive.
Taste—Slightly acrid.
Habitat—Singly or in groups on the ground in moist woods in August and September.
Notes—Closely resembles *L. uvicus,* a poisonous species with white latex becoming lilac-colored. The yellow, viscid, hairy cap is distinctive, as well as the latex turning lilac color when exposed to air.

Lactarius representaneus

19. Lactarius rufus
Poisonous. Spores white. ───────────────────────────────

Cap—1-1/2 to 4 inches wide. Convex, becoming depressed to infundibuliform with an umbo. Bay-red to rufous, not fading with age. Dry, not zoned, at first slightly woolly, soon smooth, margin inrolled early, expanded later.
Gills—Slightly decurrent, close, narrow, earth color becoming rufous, sometimes forked.
Flesh—Thin, whitish, rather soft, tinged pink. Latex white.
Stem—2 to 3-1/2 inches long, 1/4 to 1/2 inch thick. Equal, dry, smooth, slightly hairy at the base. Same color as the cap or paler. Stuffed then hollow with age.
Annulus—None.
Volva—None.
Odor—None.
Taste—Very acrid.
Habitat—Singly or in groups on the ground, especially in spruce bogs and in conifer woods, from July through September.
Notes—The very acrid latex renders this mushroom inedible as well as poisonous. This species contains Group F toxins (refer to Chapter 3).

Lactarius rufus

20. Lactarius scrobiculatus
Inedible. Spores white.

Cap—2 to 6 inches wide. Convex, becoming depressed to infundibuliform. Pale yellow to brownish yellow, sometimes reddish yellow. Varies from slightly to strongly zoned, viscid, slightly hairy at the margin, becoming smooth with age, margin at first inrolled then spreading.
Gills—Adnate to slightly decurrent, crowded, narrow, sometimes forked near the stem, whitish to yellowish color.
Flesh—Firm, white, becoming yellow when cut or bruised. Latex white, changing quickly to sulphur yellow.
Stem—1 to 3 inches long, 1/2 to 1 inch thick, equal, smooth, same color as the cap or paler, with brighter colored depressed spots, hollow.
Annulus—None.
Volva—None.
Odor—Not distinctive.
Taste—Acrid.
Habitat—Singly or in groups on the ground in moist woods, usually conifers, in August and September.
Notes—The hairy margin of the cap and the depressed brightly colored spots on the stem are distinctive. It is inedible because of the acrid latex, which turns yellow when exposed to the air.

Lactarius scrobiculatus 73

21. Lactarius torminosus
Woolly milky cap; <u>poisonous</u>. Spores white._____

Cap—1-1/2 to 4 inches wide. Fleshy, firm, convex, depressed in the center, becoming flattened, nearly infundibuliform. Pale yellow-buff to rosy flesh color, often with deeply colored zones. Viscid, smooth at the center, margin inrolled with persistent, long, whitish, woolly hairs.
Gills—Decurrent, close, narrow, whitish to yellowish, tinged with pink when old, sometimes forked near the stem.
Flesh—Firm, white to pale flesh color. Latex white, unchanging.
Stem—1 to 2-1/2 inches long, 1/2 to 3/4 inch thick. Equal or slightly tapering downward, smooth, paler color than the cap, sometimes with faint yellow spots, becoming hollow with age.
Annulus—None.
Volva—None.
Odor—Not distinctive.
Taste—Very acrid.
Habitat—Singly or in groups on the ground in woods from July to September.
Notes—The pale yellow cap and hairy inrolled margin, along with the white, unchanging, very acrid latex are distinctive.

Lactarius torminosus 75

GENUS LEPIOTA

This white-spored genus contains many species, but only one common enough in Alaska to be included in this book. The gills are free from the stem and there is a free annulus that generally hangs loose on the stem, but no volva, as in the closely related *Amanita*. Another closely related genus, the *Limacella,* has viscid caps, whereas those of *Lepiota* are dry.

22. Lepiota clypeolaria
Edibility unknown; may be poisonous. Spores white.

Cap—1 to 2 inches wide. Acorn-shaped at first, covered with a thin layer of buff-yellow or brownish tissue, expanding to bell-shaped-convex, with the outer tissue breaking into scales of creamy white to brown, the exposed flesh between the scales whitish. Frequently umbonate, smooth, brownish, becoming flattened and the scales almost disappearing with age. Margin often ragged with fragments of the veil, striate.
Gills—Free, close, slightly broad, white, edges somewhat woolly.
Flesh—Thin, soft, white color.
Stem—1-1/2 to 4 inches long and about 1/8 inch thick, tapering slightly upward. Hollow, whitish, silky feeling, sheathed with whitish cottony fibrils which may partly disappear.
Annulus—White, woolly, disappearing with age.
Volva—None.
Odor—Not distinctive.
Taste—Not distinctive.
Habitat—Singly or in groups on the ground in open woods and fields from August to October.
Notes—Suspected of being poisonous. A small mushroom of not much value as food.

Lepiota clypeolaria 77

GENUS LEUCOPAXILLUS (CLITOCYBE)

This genus is difficult to distinguish except through microscopic characters. The species are mostly whitish or dull-colored with fairly large caps and fleshy stems. Attachment of the gills varies from decurrent to sinuate. The genus closely resembles *Tricholoma* and *Clitocybe*. *Leucopaxillus* (*Clitocybe*) *giganteus* was formerly placed in the genus *Clitocybe*. The spore color is white.

23. Leucopaxillus (Clitocybe) giganteus
Edible. Spores white.

Cap—4 to 12 inches wide. Convex to flattened, becoming depressed, and finally infundibuliform. Mostly dry but may be slightly moist; smooth, slightly hairy at the margin. Whitish to buff or tan. Margin inrolled becoming spreaded and ribbed, frequently splitting.

Gills—Slightly decurrent, crowded, whitish becoming dark or dingy with age, easily separable from the flesh of the cap.

Flesh—Thick, firm, becoming softer with age, whitish color.

Stem—1-3/4 to 3 inches long, 3/4 to 2 inches thick. Short, stout, swollen, almost bulbous at the base, whitish like the cap, smooth, solid.

Annulus—None.

Volva—None.

Odor—Not distinctive.

Taste—Mild.

Habitat—Singly or in groups on the ground in mixed woods or in open places from August to October.

Notes—A very large mushroom. Easily recognized by its buff-tan-colored cap with crowded gills and short stubby stem. Pick only the young specimens for food. The mature mushrooms may be slightly tough as well as insect infested.

Leucopaxillus (Clitocybe) giganteus

GENUS LIMACELLA

This white-spored genus is similar to the *Lepiota,* but mainly differentiated by its usually viscid cap and sometimes equally viscid stems. The gills are free, and there is a free annulus on the stem. Both *Limacella* and *Lepiota* are closely related to the *Amanita* group of mushrooms, and caution should be exercised in eating any of these.

24. Limacella illinita
Edibility unknown. Spores white.

Cap—1-3/4 to 2-1/2 inches wide. White, egg-shaped becoming belllike then flattened with an umbo, glutinous, smooth, sometimes pale yellowish on the disk.
Gills—Free, close, broad, white color.
Flesh—Thin, white, soft.
Stem—2 to 3-1/2 inches long, 1/8 to 1/4 inch thick. Equal or tapering slightly upward. White. Glutinous below the annulus, silky above; hollow with age.
Annulus—Fibrillose, soon disappearing.
Volva—None.
Odor—None.
Taste—None.
Habitat—Singly or in groups on the ground in mixed woods in September and October.
Notes—The very glutinous white cap and stem and the free gills distinguish this mushroom. Sometimes the gluten is so thick that it drips from the cap. It is inedible or at least unpalatable to most people.

Limacella illinita 81

GENUS MARASMIUS

This is a large genus of white-spored mushrooms of mostly small size with the ability to shrivel up during dry periods and revive during wet. Only one, *Marasmius oreades,* the fairy ring mushroom, is of any size. Most species of the *Marasmius* are attractive but of little food value.

25. Marasmius androsaceus
Edibility unknown. Spores white.

Cap—Very small, 1/4 to 1/2 inch wide. Rounded, then flattened. Buff, reddish brown or tinged purplish. Radiately wrinkled, smooth.
Gills—Adnate, distant. Buff or flesh color.
Flesh—Thin, white.
Stem—1-1/8 to 3 inches long, 1/64 inch thick. Equal, tubular-tough, blackish, smooth.
Annulus—None.
Volva—None.
Odor—None.
Taste—Not distinctive.
Habitat—Singly and in groups on fallen leaves and other forest humus; common from July to September.
Notes—Too small to be considered of any value for food.

Marasmius androsaceus

26. Marasmius epiphyllus
Edibility unknown. Spores white.

Cap—Very small, 1/8 to 1/4 inch wide. Convex to flattened or slightly umbilicate, white, wrinkled, smooth.
Gills—Adnate, very distant, white.
Flesh—Thin, white.
Stem—1 to 1-1/2 inches long, 1/64 inch thick. Red-brown, whitish at the top, hairy at the base.
Annulus—None.
Volva—None.
Odor—None.
Taste—Not distinctive.
Habitat—Scattered, singly or in groups on fallen leaves in deciduous woods from September and October. Usually attached to the leaf at midvein.
Notes—Too small to be considered of any value for food.

Marasmius epiphyllus

GENUS MYCENA

Another large and complex group of small mushrooms generally too little to be of much use as food. The *Mycenas* are white-spored, and have fleshy, fragile or membranous caps and cartilaginous stems. Only one, *Mycena pura*, is of any interest to the mycophagist; the rest of the genus is identified mainly through microscopic characteristics.

27. Mycena pura
Edibility questionable; edible
for some persons, but not all. Spores white.

Cap—1/2 to 1-1/2 inches wide. Convex to expanded, smooth, sometimes umbonate, glabrous, moist, translucent-striate on the margin. Color varies from rosy red to violet, or shades of grayish violet, sometimes nearly white.
Gills—Adnate to sinuate, broad, moderately close, interveined, whitish, more often tinged the color of the cap.
Flesh—Moderately thick, tinged the color of the cap.
Stem—1-1/2 to 3 inches long 1/8 to 1/4 inch thick. Equal, hollow, smooth, colored as the cap or paler, sometimes twisted and striated.
Annulus—None.
Volva—None.
Odor—Radishlike.
Taste—Radishlike.
Habitat—Singly or in groups on the ground in open woods, from June or July through September or October.
Notes—This is one of the larger species of the genus, but generally considered to be a bit small for food. Early investigators considered it poisonous, or at least a sickener, and some people may react if eating a great deal of it.

Mycena pura 87

GENUS PLEUROTUS

This white-spored genus is characterized by mushrooms having excentric or lateral stems, or lacking stems altogether (sessile). Most species occur on dead or decaying wood of stumps and trees, either singly or more frequently in shelflike clusters. There are no poisonous species known to exist in the genus *Pleurotus*.

28. Pleurotus (Pleurotellus) porrigens
Angel wings; edible. Spores white.———————————————————

Cap—1/2 to 3 inches long, to 2 inches wide. Sessile, elongated, laterally attached, margin inrolled, later flattening, narrowing toward the base, mostly fan- or ear-shaped. White, watery, slightly striate on the margin when moist, sometimes lobed, smooth to slightly hairy at the base.
Gills—Mostly reaching the base point of attachment, close, narrow, linear, white or cream color, sometimes forking near the base.
Flesh—Thin, white, fragile.
Stem—Sessile.
Annulus—None.
Volva—None.
Odor—Mild.
Taste—Mild.
Habitat—In overlapping shelflike clusters on decaying wood, usually conifers in September and October.
Notes—A small but delicious species. May be mistaken for other species of *Pleurotus,* but all are edible and harmless unless old and decaying.

Pleurotus (Pleurotellus) porrigens

29. Pleurotus (Panellus) serotinus
Oyster mushroom; edible. Spores white.

Cap—Compact, 1 to 3 inches wide, more or less semicircular or kidney-shaped, convex, with inrolled margin, becoming somewhat flattened, varying from densely hairy to smooth, slimy-viscid when wet. Olivaceous or yellow-green to dull brown or reddish.
Gills—Narrowly adnate, a sharp line between the end of the gills and the stem, thin, close, narrow at each end, whitish to yellowish tan.
Flesh—Thick, white, firm.
Stem—Solid, short and stubby. 1/4 to 3/4 inch long, to 3/8 inch thick, laterally attached, continuous with the cap on its upper surface, hairy below, sparsely dotted with minute dark brown scales, yellowish.
Annulus—None.
Volva—None.
Odor—Not distinctive.
Taste—Not distinctive.
Habitat—Solitary or more often in overlapping clusters on wood of deciduous trees such as cottonwood and alder, from August to November.
Notes—Sometimes found late in the fall. Rather tough and leathery when mature. A good edible species when young and fresh.

Pleurotus (Panellus) serotinus

GENUS RUSSULA

This genus is similar to *Lactarius,* but has no latex and the flesh is generally more fragile and brittle. It is a large and important genus, but one difficult to identify exactly without mistakes. The spore color is mostly white, but some species will have spores that vary from creamy or pale yellow to light ocher. The exact spore color is very important in identifying the species, and a spore print should be made of every specimen collected. The caps are usually brightly colored in shades of red, yellow, purple, green or bluish, although some will be dull colors of white or brown. The caps may be dry or viscid, smooth, scaly or hairy. The taste will vary from mild, bitter, extremely acrid to nauseous, and these factors should be noted in young fresh specimens in the field.

30. Russula aeruginea
Edible. Spores white or creamy white.

Cap—1-1/2 to 3 inches wide. Convex to flattened, slightly depressed in the center. Dull to dark smoky green, darker in the center, sometimes tinged brownish, paler on the margin. Viscid when wet, velvety when dry, firm, becoming fragile. Peel is separable only at the margin; margin even or striate with age.
Gills—Adnate to almost free, moderately close, narrow, equal, sometimes interspaced with a few shorter gills, white to cream color.
Flesh—Thick on the cap, thin at the margin, white or slightly greenish, ashy under the peel, fragile.
Stem—1-1/2 to 2 inches long, 1/4 to 1/2 inch thick. Nearly equal or tapering slightly downward, smooth, white, firm, stuffed.
Annulus—None.
Volva—None.
Odor—Mild.
Taste—Mild.
Habitat—Solitary or in groups on the ground of mixed woods from July to September.
Notes—The green color, creamy white spores and mild taste are characteristic for this species.

Russula aeruginea

31. Russula brevipes
Edible. Spores white.

Cap—3 to 8 inches wide. Convex, depressed in the center, dry, slightly woolly. White or stained grayish to black. Margin inrolled then expanded, not striate.
Gills—Decurrent, close, sometimes forked with veins between; white, or stained cinnamon or brownish.
Flesh—Firm, white, fragile.
Stem—1-1/4 to 4 inches long, 1 to 1-1/8 inches thick. Equal, dry, smooth. Whitish with brown stains.
Annulus—None.
Volva—None.
Odor—Somewhat disagreeable.
Taste—Slightly acrid.
Habitat—Singly or scattered in groups on the ground under conifers or in mixed woods from July to October.
Notes—The slightly acrid property is said to disappear upon cooking. This mushroom is quite common in Alaska and you should eat but a little of it at first to see if it agrees with your digestion.

Russula brevipes

32. Russula claroflava (flava)
Yellow russula; edible. Spores pale yellow.————————————

Cap—2-1/2 to 5 inches wide. Convex, flattened. Bright chrome or lemon yellow. Margin slightly striate.
Gills—Adnate. Whitish to primrose color. Broad, moderately close.
Flesh—Firm, fragile, whitish, slowly turning gray where bruised.
Stem—2-3/4 to 4 inches long, 3/4 to 1 inch thick. Equal, slightly veined longitudinally. Whitish, turning slowly gray where bruised.
Annulus—None.
Volva—None.
Odor—Not distinctive.
Taste—Mild.
Habitat—Singly or in groups on soggy ground in birch forests or mixed woods from late August to October.
Notes—The fragile, crumbling flesh, bright yellow cap and its association with birch distinguishes this species. Cook as you would any edible *Russula*.

Russula claroflava (flava)

33. Russula densifolia
Edible. Spores white.

Cap—2 to 4 inches wide. Convex to umbilicate, becoming flattened, usually depressed, firm and rigid. Dull whitish becoming smoky brown. Slightly viscid, smooth, margin even.
Gills—Adnate to decurrent, close, narrow, whitish or grayish, becoming reddish where bruised, then turning black.
Flesh—Thick, firm, white, turning reddish, then black where bruised.
Stem—1-3/4 to 2-1/2 inches long, 1/2 to 1 inch thick, equal or tapering downward; smooth, solid. Whitish, becoming reddish then black where bruised.
Annulus—None.
Volva—None.
Odor—Not distinctive.
Taste—Mild to slowly or slightly acrid, especially the gills.
Habitat—Solitary or in groups on the ground in woods from July to September.
Notes—Unattractive in appearance. Distinguished by its staining reddish to black where bruised. This is a slow process and must be watched for carefully. Old specimens may be deteriorated sufficiently to place them in the Group F toxins, as would many edible species if eaten in any stage of decomposition.

Russula densifolia

34. Russula emetica
Emetic russula; inedible and
dangerous; <u>may be poisonous.</u> Spores white.

Cap—2 to 4 inches wide. Fleshy, firm, becoming fragile, convex to flattened or slightly depressed. Rosy to blood-red, fading to whitish. Viscid when wet, smooth, shining; peel separates readily, margin strongly striated.
Gills—Slightly adnexed to free, close, broad, narrow near the stem; white color.
Flesh—White, red under the peel; fragile.
Stem—1-1/2 to 3 inches long, 1/2 to 3/4 inch thick. Nearly equal, smooth. White to tinged red. Spongy, stuffed.
Annulus—None.
Volva—None.
Odor—Not distinctive.
Taste—Very acrid.
Habitat—Singly or in scattered groups on the ground or on very rotten wood from July to October.
Notes—As the name implies, it acts as a purgative. The taste is very acrid, but some investigators claim that it disappears with cooking. It is not recommended as edible because it contains the Group F toxins.

Russula emetica 101

35. Russula foetens
Fetid russula; inedible and
dangerous; may be poisonous. Spores white.

Cap—2-1/2 to 5 inches wide. Firm, becoming fragile; rounded, becoming expanded and flattened to slightly depressed. Yellowish to dingy brown. Smooth, viscid; peel separable part way from the margin to the disk; margin coarsely striated.
Gills—Adnexed, close, broad; whitish, becoming yellowish with age, dingy where bruised; exuding water drops when young, occasionally forked.
Flesh—Thin, fragile, dingy white to yellowish under the peel.
Stem—1 to 3 inches long, 1/2 to 1 inch thick. Equal, smooth. White to dingy brown in age or where bruised. Stuffed, becoming hollow in age.
Annulus—None.
Volva—None.
Odor—Strong, resembles bitter almonds, then fetid.
Taste—Very acrid.
Habitat—Singly or in groups on the ground in mixed woods from July to September.
Notes—The dingy colors and the unpleasant smell make this an extremely unattractive mushroom. It falls into Group F mushroom toxins, but because of the odor and taste is not likely to be eaten anyway.

Russula foetens

36. Russula xerampelina
Woodland russula; edible. Spores pale yellow._____

Cap—2 to 4 inches wide, firm, convex to flattened, slightly depressed. Color varies from reddish purple on the margin to olive-green in the center, mixed with brownish purple or olivaceous. Dry, smooth, peel difficult to separate from the flesh; margin even.
Gills—Adnexed, close, narrower at the stem, some forked; pale cream color or yellow.
Flesh—White, pinkish under the peel.
Stem—1-1/2 to 3 inches long, 1/2 to 1 inch thick. Equal, smooth, may be slightly wrinkled. White to reddish and becoming dingy olivaceous yellow when handled or with age. Solid, somewhat spongy.
Annulus—None.
Volva—None.
Odor—Disagreeable, somewhat fishlike with age or upon drying.
Taste—Mild.
Habitat—Singly or scattered on the ground, mostly in woods from August to October.
Notes—The fishy odor upon drying may deter some people from eating this mushroom but it is nonpcisonous. Select only young specimens for the table, leaving the old for reseeding.

Russula xerampelina

GENUS TRICHOLOMA

A large and complex group of white-spored mushrooms that grow only on the ground and often appear late in the season. They have fleshy stems, gills adnate to sinuate and frequently notched at the stem. There is no volva or annulus. Only those edible species that can be positively identified should be collected for food.

37. Tricholoma aurantium
Edibility unknown. Spores white.

Cap—1 to 3 inches wide. Convex, becoming flattened, slightly umbonate. Reddish brown to orange-red. Viscid, becoming scaly; margin woolly, glutinous, inrolled becoming elevated with age.
Gills—Adnexed, close. Whitish, becoming spotted and staining a rusty brown. A few forked.
Flesh—Thick on the disk, thin on the margin, white.
Stem—1-1/2 to 2-1/2 inches long, 1/4 to 1/2 inch thick. Equal, sometimes narrower at the base. More or less covered with rings of scales colored as the cap reaching up to an obscure annular zone; white near the cap and between scales. Solid.
Annulus—None.
Volva—None.
Odor—Farinaceous (mealy).
Taste—Not distinctive.
Habitat—Singly or in groups on the ground in woods and open fields from August to October.
Notes—The bright color of the cap and scaly stem with gills staining brown are the distinguishing features of this mushroom. Its edibility is not known, but one suspects that it will agree with most people. Eat only a small bit at first.

Tricholoma aurantium 107

38. Tricholoma flavovirens
Man on horseback; edible. Spores white._____

Cap—2 to 4 inches wide. Compact, fleshy, round becoming flattened. Pale to bright yellow, usually stained reddish or brownish. Viscid, smooth, may be faintly scaly; margin incurved becoming elevated.
Gills—Free, rounded at the stem, broad, close; sulphur yellow color.
Flesh—Whitish or tinged yellow.
Stem—1 to 2-1/2 inches long, 1/4 to 3/4 inch thick. Stout, equal or slightly thicker at the base. Whitish to pale yellow. Solid, smooth, sometimes slightly scaly.
Annulus—None.
Volva—None.
Odor—Not distinctive.
Taste—Slightly unpleasant when raw.
Habitat—In groups mostly on the ground in conifer woods from August to October.
Notes—A very popular mushroom in Alaska. The yellow viscid cap and yellow gills staining reddish brown are distinctive characteristics.

Tricholoma flavovirens

39. Tricholoma imbricatum
Brick top or shingled tricholoma; edibility unknown. Spores white.

Cap—2 to 4 inches wide. Conical, dry, peel breaking into coarse imbricating scales. Reddish brown. Margin remains mostly incurved.
Gills—Adnate. Whitish, becoming rufous-spotted with age. Close, moderately broad.
Flesh—Firm, whitish, tinged slightly reddish.
Stem—2 to 4 inches long, 1/4 to 1/2 inch thick. About equal, a bit thicker at the base. Pale reddish brown. Solid, minutely striated, somewhat rooting.
Annulus—None.
Volva—None.
Odor—Faintly mealy.
Taste—Not distinctive.
Habitat—Singly or in groups on the ground in mixed woods from August to October.
Notes—Because the edibility is relatively unknown you should try this mushroom with caution. Eat a small amount and wait 24 hours. It is probably edible for most people.

Tricholoma imbricatum 111

40. Tricholoma sulphureum
Sulphur tricholoma; inedible and dangerous. Spores white.————

Cap—1 to 3-1/2 inches wide. Convex, becoming flattened, slightly umbonate; bright sulphur yellow, often tinged with brown at the center; smooth and dry, not viscid.
Gills—Attached and toothed, subdistant, thick, broad, sulphur yellow.
Flesh—Firm, fibrous, yellow, or pale greenish yellow.
Stem—3 to 4-1/2 inches long, 1/4 to 1/2 inch thick. Slender, fibrous, equal, becoming squat at the base, sulphur yellow color, with longitudinal striations, stuffed, becoming hollow.
Annulus—None.
Volva—None.
Odor—Strong creosote or sulfur dioxide smell.
Taste—Repugnant.
Habitat—Singly or in groups, sometimes in small clusters on the ground in mixed woods from August to October.
Notes—The gassy odor and putrid taste is enough to deter anyone from attempting to eat this mushroom.

Tricholoma sulphureum 113

41. Tricholoma terreum
Gray agaric, earth-colored tricholoma; edible. Spores white.───────

Cap—1 to 2-1/2 inches wide. Convex to flattened, subumbonate. Gray or house mouse-colored. Dry, fibrillose becoming scaly to slightly woolly, scales dark gray to sooty.
Gills—Adnexed, close, broad, white to dingy.
Flesh—Thin, white, fragile, grayish beneath the peel.
Stem—1 to 2 inches long, 1/8 to 1/4 inch thick. Equal, solid, white to grayish color.
Annulus—none.
Volva—None.
Taste—Mild.
Odor—Mild.
Habitat—Singly or in groups and clusters of several on the ground in open woods from July to October.
Notes—A bit tough, but cooks in an hour with fair flavor.

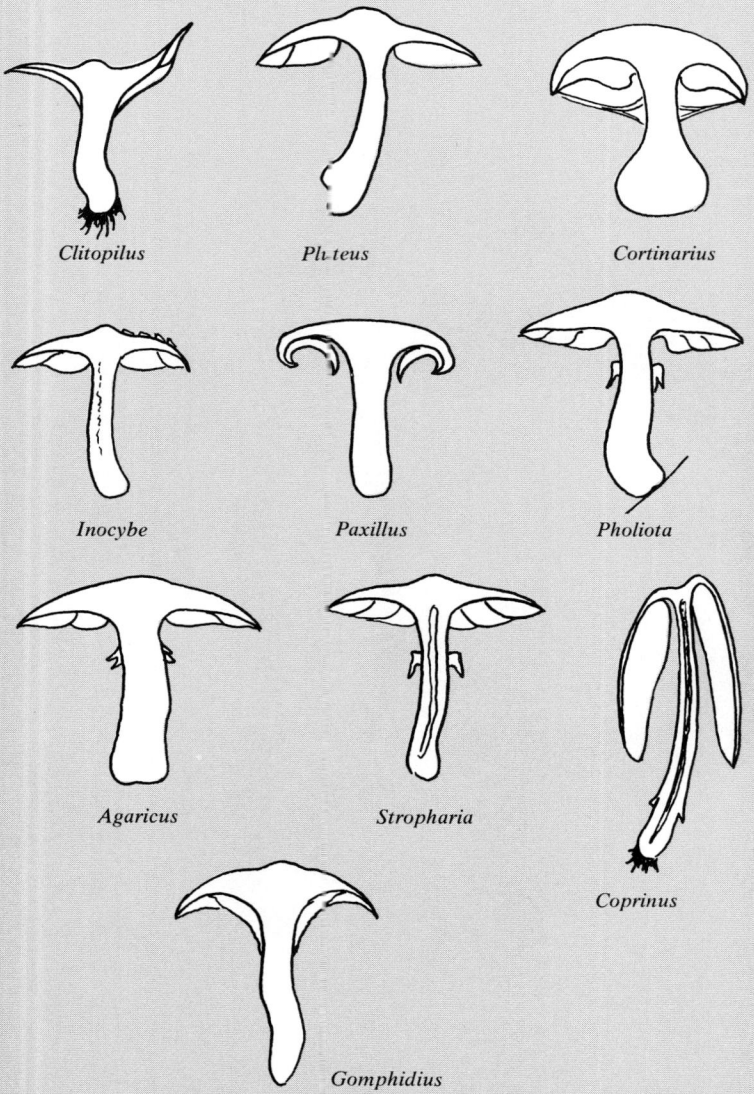

Figure 6—Gilled Mushrooms—Family *Agaricaceae*—With Spores NOT Colorless, White, Cream, Yellow or Buff

Chapter 6
Gilled Mushrooms Part Two

Family Agaricaceae With Spores NOT Colorless, White, Cream, Yellow or Buff

This chapter includes descriptions of 25 species of the family *Agaricaceae* (color plate numbers 42 through 66) representing the following 13 genera:

Clitopilus
Pluteus
Cortinarius
Gomphus (*Neurophyllum*)
Inocybe
Paxillus
Pholiota

Agaricus
Naematoloma
Stropharia
Rozites (*Pholiota*)
Coprinus
Gomphidius

Cross sections of typical mushrooms are shown in Figure 6.
To be sure of identifying mushrooms correctly, use the keys given in Chapter 4.

GENUS CLITOPILUS

This genus has a pink spore color, gills broadly adnate to decurrent, with fleshy to fibrous stems having the same texture as the caps, and not separating readily from it. There is no volva or annulus. *Clitopilus prunulus* is the type species for the genus.

42. Clitopilus prunulus
Plum agaric; edible. Spores pink.

Cap—1 to 5 inches wide. Convex becoming flattened, sometimes almost funnel-shaped, margin inrolled but becoming elevated and wavy with age. Dry, felty, or somewhat velvety to the touch, may be slightly viscid in damp air. White to ash gray. Usually covered with scurfy particles that fall off, but may remain along the margin.
Gills—Decurrent, separated, may be interspaced with smaller gills, broad, often curved, whitish to pale pink with age.
Flesh—White, tender and fragile.
Stem—1/2 to 2-1/2 inches long, 1/4 to 1/2 inch thick. Equal or nearly so, dry, soft. Dull white. Upper surface covered with scurfy particles below the gills; the base is somewhat cottony, may have longitudinal striations.
Annulus—None.
Volva—None.
Odor—Of flour or meal.
Taste—As flour, sometimes turns bitter.
Habitat—Singly or in groups on the ground in mixed woods, clearings and shady meadows from August to October.
Notes—Very common, an excellent eating mushroom, cooks quickly. Sometimes mistaken for the uncommon *Clitocybe dealbata,* a poisonous species with white spores and a fibrous consistency.

Clitopilus prunulus

GENUS PLUTEUS

Another pink-spored genus of mushrooms that is distinguished by its gills free from the stem which is easily separable from the cap. There is no annulus or volva. *Pluteus* usually occurs on old stumps and logs, or on some form of decayed wood. All are typically soft in consistency and decay rapidly with age. Except for the common *Pluteus cervinus,* most are too small to be of much food value.

43. Pluteus cervinus
Deer mushroom, fawn-colored agaric; edible. Spores pink or brownish salmon.

Cap—1-1/2 to 4 inches wide. Soft and fleshy, convex becoming flattened, sometimes with a broad umbo, smooth, dryish. Drab coloration varying from a dull dark brown to pale dingy fawn, darkest on the top, paler near the margin, sometimes streaked with darker fibrils, fading with age. Margin even.

Gills—Free, close, broad, rounded next to the stem, soft. White, turning flesh pink to flesh tan.

Flesh—White, thick toward the disk, very thin at the margin.

Stem—2 to 6 inches long, 1/4 to 1/2 inch thick. Enlarged slightly downward, solid, smooth, whitish or tinged yellow or brownish, often with scattered fibrils.

Annulus—None.

Volva—None.

Odor—Mild, like raw potato.

Taste—Mild to somewhat disagreeable.

Habitat—Singly or in groups of several on decaying stumps and logs or buried roots in deciduous or mixed woods from June to September, or later when climate is mild.

Notes—A well-known, good edible mushroom. Collect the young specimens and leave the old for reseeding.

Pluteus cervinus

GENUS CORTINARIUS

This is a large genus containing several hundred species. The principal distinguishing characteristic is the cobwebby cortina or veil that covers the gills in the young mushrooms. It appears as a loose, silky, threadlike or cobwebby mass that may persist as a ring or annular zone on the stem, or disappear as the mushroom ages. The spore color is dark to rusty yellow-brown. The gills of the mature mushroom are usually stained dark brown from the spores, but in the younger stages may vary in color from white to yellow, olivaceous or lilac. Some of the *Cortinarii* are suspected of causing illness, and some are unpleasant to the taste.

44. Cortinarius cinnamomeus
Cinnamon cortinarius; edible but only with caution.
Spores yellow-brown (rusty).────────────────────────

Cap—2 to 4 inches wide. Convex becoming flattened in age, dry. Yellow-brown, olive-brown to cinnamon color. With cobwebby veil when young, margin inrolled becoming elevated.
Gills—Adnate, close, olive-yellow to cinnamon, broad, hidden in the young buttons by a cobwebby veil.
Flesh—Thin, yellowish to olive-yellow.
Stem—3 to 4 inches long, 1/8 to 1/4 inch thick. Equal, dry, often curved, finely hairy, yellow to cinnamon-buff color.
Annulus—An inconspicuous hairy ring left from the cobwebby veil that breaks as the mushroom matures.
Volva—None.
Odor—Not distinctive.
Taste—Not distinctive.
Habitat—Singly or in close groups on the ground in conifer woods from July to September.
Notes—To be avoided. The eating quality is mediocre. It is very similar to *C. semisanguineus* of which the edibility is unknown. Other *Cortinarii* are known to be poisonous or at least sickeners.

Cortinarius cinnamomeus 123

45. Cortinarius collinitus
Edible. Spores yellow-brown (rusty).

Cap—1-1/4 to 3 inches wide. Convex to flattened, fleshy. Sometimes whitish when young, becoming yellowish to orange-yellow in color. Very viscid when moist, margin incurved early with a cobwebby veil, becoming elevated with age.
Gills—Adnate with a tooth; close, broad. Pale violet, turning dull reddish brown with age. Hidden when young with a cobwebby veil.
Flesh—Whitish to a pale yellowish buff.
Stem—2-1/2 to 4-1/2 inches long, 3/4 to 1-1/4 inches thick. Equal or tapering slightly downward, stuffed, viscid; covered with a pale violaceous to whitish universal veil which, when it cracks, leaves thickish irregular bands or patches. At first whitish, becoming stained rusty or yellowish toward the base, the upper portion is whitish and silky.
Annulus—A collapsed inconspicuous ring.
Volva—None.
Odor—Mild.
Taste—Mild.
Habitat—Usually found in groups on the ground in mixed woods from August to October.
Notes—Fairly easy to recognize because of the yellowish viscid cap and stem, and whitish or pale violet patches on the stem. Wash and wipe off the viscid layer before cooking.

Cortinarius collinitus

46. Cortinarius semisanguineus
Edibility unknown; probably edible. Spores yellow-brown (rusty).———

Cap—3/4 to 2-1/2 inches wide. Convex becoming flattened, sometimes umbonate. Tawny yellow to cinnamon-yellow. Silky to the touch, minutely scaled, margin even, sometimes splitting.
Gills—Adnate to decurrent, crowded, narrow, blood-red color, hidden by cobwebby veil in young plants.
Flesh—Thin, yellowish.
Stem—1 to 2-1/2 inches long, 1/8 to 1/4 inch thick, equal, yellow to tawny, solid.
Annulus—Inconspicuous or absent.
Volva—None.
Odor—Mild.
Taste—Mild.
Habitat—In groups on the ground in moist woods from August to October.
Notes—Similar to *C. cinnamomeus* except for yellowish cap and stem, and the blood-red gills, which are distinctive for this species. Other *Cortinarii* are known to be poisonous or at least sickeners.

47. Cortinarius traganus
Edibility unknown. Spores yellow-brown (rusty). _____

Cap—1-1/2 to 4 inches wide. Convex becoming flattened, somewhat umbonate in age, dry, pale lilac overall, sometimes cracked when old.
Gills—Attached, separate, broad, pale lilac when young, becoming spore-stained yellow-brown with age, hidden by a cobwebby veil in the young mushroom.
Flesh—Thick, firm, yellowish.
Stem—1-1/2 to 3 inches long, 1/2 to 1 inch thick, enlarging to a club-shaped bulb at the base, dry. Pale lilac above and below hairy ring.
Annulus—Hairy, inconspicuous, left from thick cobwebby, whitish, tinted lilac veil.
Volva—none.
Odor—Pungent, may be disagreeable to some.
Taste—Not distinctive.
Habitat—Singly, mostly in groups on the ground in old coniferous woods, often in deep moss, from August to October.
Notes—Suspect edible, but it may disagree with some people's digestion.

Cortinarius traganus

48. Cortinarius violaceus
Violet cortinarius; edible. Spores yellow-brown (rusty).——————

Cap—2 to 5 inches wide, convex becoming flattened and slightly umbonate, fleshy, dark violet color, sometimes metallic-shiny, covered with small erect tufts or scales, margin somewhat fringed, universal veil inconspicuous.
Gills—Adnate, broad, distant, dark violet color.
Flesh—Thick, firm, grayish violet to dark violet, not turning purple when bruised.
Stem—2-1/2 to 5 inches long, 1/2 to 1 inch thick, wider below, somewhat bulbous, dark violet out, violaceous within.
Annulus—Inconspicuous or absent.
Volva—None.
Odor—Mild.
Taste—Mild.
Habitat—Singly or scattered on the ground, usually in coniferous woods, from August to October.
Notes—Distinguished by the dark violet cap and gills, and somewhat scaly cap. A very picturesque mushroom of good texture and flavor. Pick only the young specimens, because they tend to become infested with insects when mature.

Cortinarius violaceus

GENUS GOMPHUS (NEUROPHYLLUM)

This genus is characterized by clublike or vaselike caps which may be depressed or hollow. The gills are more like wrinkled and irregular ridges which are almost poroid at times. *Gomphus* are closely related to the chantarelles (*Cantharellus* species).

49. Gomphus clavatus (Neurophyllum clavatum)
Clustered chantarelle; edible when young.
Spores pale ocher or yellowish orange. _____

Cap—1-1/2 to 4 inches wide. Flat to club-shaped, dry, minutely scaled, margin lobed. Light purple to faded purplish brown. Sometimes the cap is funnel-form.
Gills—Extend down the stem to the base. Blunt, thick, interconnected by veins, frequently forked. Light purple to purplish brown.
Flesh—Firm, whitish or tinged cinnamon color.
Stem—1/4 to 2 inches long, 1/4 to 3/4 inch thick. Usually expanding from a compound base blending into the funnel-shaped cap. Same color as the cap and gills but darker purple at the smooth base, which is usually covered with whitish mycelium.
Annulus—None.
Volva—None.
Odor—Almond smell.
Taste—Very pleasant when young, very acid when the mushroom matures or gets old.
Habitat—Singly, in groups and sometimes clustered on the ground in rows and rings and on stumps of dead trees from August to October.
Notes—Pick only young specimens for cooking. Cook slowly over a low fire to attain flavor and tenderness. The edibility of old specimens is uncertain because of their acidity.

Gomphus clavatus (Neurophyllum clavatum)

GENUS INOCYBE

This genus is difficult to identify positively except by specific microscopic characters. Most species are small and not much value as food, and the edibility of many is unknown. The spore color is mainly ocher-brown in mass. The caps are usually dull-colored, conic to campanulate, more or less scaly and frequently split radially.

50. Inocybe lacera
Poisonous. Spores yellow-brown.

Cap—3/4 to 1-1/2 inches wide. Convex to umbonate. Cigar brown color, sometimes olive-tinged at the faintly striated margin.
Gills—Adnate, broad, distant, pale olive-gray, becoming dingy olive-brown.
Flesh—Thin, whitish to a pale dingy gray.
Stem—1-1/2 to 3 inches long, 1/8 to 1/4 inch thick, tapering downward, rusty brown color.
Annulus—None.
Volva—None.
Odor—Not distinctive.
Taste—Not distinctive.
Habitat—Singly or in groups on the ground, mostly in sandy or gravelly places in mixed woods, mostly coniferous, from July to October.
Notes—Most investigators list this as an unknown, but some list it as poisonous or at least a sickener. It is too small to be of much value as food. It may accidentally be mistaken for others of the genus, some of which are very poisonous.

Inocybe lacera 135

GENUS PAXILLUS

This genus is distinguished by its ocher-yellow-brown spores, a stem that is more or less excentric, and gills that are slightly decurrent and interlaced to the stem, sometimes becoming poroid and easily separable from the flesh of the cap. *Paxillus* is a relatively small genus with only two common species, neither of which is recommended for food.

51. Paxillus involutus
Involute paxillus; edible,
but not recommended. Spores yellow-brown.————————————

Cap—2 to 5 inches wide. Convex, becoming flattened then depressed. Color varies from yellowish brown to reddish brown or olive-brown with darker spots. Smooth, margin persistently inrolled and often ridged.
Gills—Decurrent, easily separable from the cap, crowded, broad, forked on the stem, olive-yellow, becoming brown when bruised.
Flesh—Thick, pale yellow, becoming brownish where bruised.
Stem—1-1/2 to 3 inches long, 1/2 to 1-1/4 inches thick. Equal to tapering slightly downward; smooth. Colored like the cap or paler, often streaked and spotted with darker brown. Solid, usually central, but sometimes excentric.
Annulus—None.
Volva—None.
Odor—None.
Taste—Not distinctive.
Habitat—Singly or in groups. On the ground in woods or at the base of old stumps from July to October.
Notes—There are reports that it has caused a number of poisonings. However, most authors list it as edible, at least with caution. It is easily recognized by its dingy coloration and the tightly inrolled margin. It is said to be insipid at its best.

Paxillus involutus 137

GENUS PHOLIOTA

This is an important genus for the mycophagist to know because it contains a number of fairly large, good, edible species often appearing in large clusters, providing abundant material for food. The spore color is ocher to rusty brown. The gills are attached to the stem, and there is a membranous annulus but no volva. Some species are scaly, but others are smooth. In some the caps and stems are viscid. They may be found mostly on wood, but sometimes on the ground. *Pholiota squarrosa* is the type species for the genus. Most are edible, but some are unpalatable, and at least one species is known to be poisonous.

52. Pholiota aurea

Golden pholiota; edibility questionable; edible for some persons, but not all. Spores yellow-brown.

Cap—4 to 12 inches wide, sometimes wider. Convex becoming expanded, slightly cracked. Golden brown color. Scurfy or granular coating rubbing off easily, slightly umbonate, margin usually has the remnants of a veil.

Gills—Adnexed, close, rounded behind, broad, clay color, becoming rusty yellow.

Flesh—Thick, firm, white to yellowish.

Stem—2-1/2 to 8 inches long, 1/2 to 1-1/2 inches thick. Equal or may be enlarged at the base, sheathed from below by a veil which breaks off at the margin of the cap and leaves a membranous ring.

Annulus—Conspicuous, large and flaring upward, then pendulous, membranous, thick, persistent. Dark buff below, lemon color above.

Volva—None.

Odor—Faintly earthy, pleasant

Taste—Not distinctive, but mild.

Habitat—Singly or in large groups on the ground in rich soil of deciduous woods, usually alder, July or August through October.

Notes—*P. aurea* has caused severe gastrointestinal upsets in some people; care should be exercised in eating it for the first time. This very large, easily recognized mushroom is very common in Alaska's Southcentral area and is readily collected. Pick only the large young buttons, some as big as baseballs, and leave the older specimens. The stems are tough. Wipe off or brush away the powdery covering before cooking.

Pholiota aurea

53. Pholiota (Kuehneromyces) mutabilis
Edible. Spores yellow-brown. _____

Cap—1 to 3 inches wide. Convex and soon flattened with a slight umbo, margin inrolled, becoming expanded, thin, sometimes cracked or split. Date brown, chamois, or ginger color when dry, frequently brick-red in the center of the cap.
Gills—Adnexed, slightly decurrent, broad, close and interspaced with smaller gills. Yellowish, then cinnamon, and finally rust-colored.
Flesh—Whitish, moderately thick, fragile.
Stem—1-1/2 to 2-1/2 inches long, 1/8 to 1/4 inch thick. Covered with dark reddish scales. Equal, often curved, stuffed, becoming hollow with age, tough.
Annulus—May be inconspicuous, colored as the cap, made up of tufts and scales, disappearing in older specimens.
Volva—None.
Odor—Faintly fruitlike, slightly medicinal.
Taste—Pleasant.
Habitat—In tufts or clumps on stumps of deciduous trees or buried wood from August to October.
Notes—Grows in enormous clusters. Discard stems as they are tough. This mushroom makes good stews and soups. It is mistaken harmlessly for species 4, *Armillariella (Armillaria) mellea,* the honey mushroom, which is also edible. However, care should be taken not to confuse it with *Galerina autumnalis,* which is viscid and definitely known to be poisonous.

Pholiota (Kuehneromyces) mutabilis

54. Pholiota squarrosa
Rough or scaly pholiota; edible. Spores yellow-brown.───────

Cap—2 to 5 inches wide. Convex, becoming expanded. Saffron yellow to tan. Covered with stiff, upturned brownish scales, becoming larger and farther apart as the cap matures, dry, not viscid.
Gills—Slightly decurrent, toothed, close, moderately broad. Pale yellow turning rusty red.
Flesh—Yellowish, tough.
Stem—1-1/2 to 3 inches long, 1/4 to 1/2 inch thick, equal, often tapering toward the base, usually flattened by the base of other specimens in the clump. Above the ring, white and smooth; below the ring, covered with like scales of the cap and similar in color; toward the base, the color darkens and the scales become smaller.
Annulus—Rather large, smooth above, scaly beneath, paler color than the cap or stem.
Volva—None.
Odor—Of decaying wood, earthy.
Taste—Earthy.
Habitat—Grows in large clumps on live or dead deciduous or coniferous trees, stumps and logs from August to October.
Notes—Mistaken harmlessly for species 4, *Armillariella* (*Armillaria*) *mellea*, the honey mushroom, also edible. Boil in water for several minutes and discard water. Use for sauces and soups. Stems are tough.

Pholiota squarrosa 143

55. Pholiota squarroso-adiposa
Fat pholiota; edible. Spores yellow-brown.—————————————————

Cap—2 to 4 inches wide. Convex to expanded, viscid, with glutinous, brownish triangular scales, golden brown color overall.
Gills—Adnexed, close, moderately broad, straw yellow turning rusty red.
Flesh—Thin, pale yellow, tough.
Stem—1-1/2 to 3 inches long, 1/4 to 1/2 inch thick, yellow, smooth above, scaly below.
Annulus—Thin, scaly, incomplete to missing in some specimens, scales yellow to tannish.
Volva—None.
Odor—Woody.
Taste—Earthy.
Habitat—In dense tufts and clusters on dead and decaying trees, stumps and logs of mixed woods from August to October.
Notes—Similar to *P. squarrosa* but very viscid. Remove slime from the caps before cooking. Boil caps for a few minutes and discard the water before cooking. The stems are tough and unpalatable. Old specimens will have a strong earthy taste.

Pholiota squarroso-adiposa

GENUS AGARICUS

This is one of the most important genera for the mushroom hunter. It includes both the commercially grown cultivated mushroom as well as the wild meadow mushroom that is most frequently collected and eaten in North America. The genus is characterized by purple-brown spores, a conspicuous annulus, and free gills. The stem is of a different consistency than the cap and readily separates from it. There is no volva. The gills are usually white at first, turning pinkish and then dark brown at maturity, due in part to the shedding spores.

56. Agaricus arvensis
Prairie or horse mushroom; edible. Spores purple-brown._____

Cap—2 to 8 inches wide, campanulate or finger-shaped, then convex, becoming flattened when fully expanded, smooth and shiny, dry to the touch. White with pale yellow patches, becoming light brown overall. Margin irregular, sometimes split, its edge the remains of a veil.
Gills—Free, rounded at both ends, broad, close and interspaced with smaller gills. White at first, turning pinkish gray, then tobacco brown in color with age.
Flesh—White, solid, tending to turn yellowish then pink.
Stem—1-1/2 to 4 inches long, 1/2 to 3/4 inch thick, equal. Whitish, becoming pale yellow to nut brown. Stuffed, becoming hollow in age.
Annulus—A full double-skirted ring, outer membranous, inner woolly with a ragged margin, white to brownish, fragile, sometimes absent in old specimens.
Volva—None.
Odor—Resembles anise.
Taste—Mild.
Habitat—Singly or in groups in grassy places on the ground of mixed woods from July to September, and sometimes October.
Notes—Excellent raw or cooked. It can also be dried or frozen. Mistaken harmlessly for *A. campestris*, also edible.

Agaricus arvensis 147

57. Agaricus campestris
Meadow mushroom; edible. Spores purple-brown.

Cap—1-1/2 to 6 inches wide. Convex then flattened, becoming plane; fleshy, firm. White, becoming brownish-tinged when old. Silky and shiny, margin extended and fringed with the remnants of a veil.
Gills—Free, crowded, narrow. Pink, becoming purple-brown and finally blackish with age.
Flesh—White, thick, firm, not changing color when bruised.
Stem—1 to 3 inches long, 1/4 to 3/4 inch thick, equal, sometimes narrower at the base, white, silky above the ring, brownish below, stuffed.
Annulus—Thin, single, white, fragile, sometimes remains attached to the margin of the cap.
Volva—None.
Odor—Pleasantly mild.
Taste—Pleasant.
Habitat—Singly or in groups on the ground in grassy places of mixed woods, open fields and meadows from July to October.
Notes—Excellent raw or cooked. It can also be dried or frozen. Similar to *A. bisporus,* the commercially grown mushroom, but superior in flavor. Mistaken harmlessly for *A. arvensis,* which is also edible.

Agaricus campestris 149

58. Agaricus meleagris (placomyces)
Scaly flat-top; edible with caution. Spores purple-brown. _____

Cap—2 to 5 inches wide. Broadly ovate, becoming convex, then flattened. Whitish beneath blackish brown fibrillose scales covering the cap.
Gills—Free, crowded, narrow. White to grayish-pinkish, turning a dark purple-brown.
Flesh—White to slightly yellowish, sometimes with a pinkish cast, thin.
Stem—2-1/2 to 5 inches long, 1/4 to 1/2 inch thick, tapering upward from a more or less bulbous base; smooth. Whitish, staining yellowish. Stuffed, becoming hollow with age.
Annulus—A large, conspicuous double ring, whitish above, the lower layer cracking into brownish patches.
Volva—None.
Odor—Slightly disagreeable, faintly phenollike.
Taste—Mild.
Habitat—Singly or in groups, sometimes clustered on the ground in mixed woods from July to September.
Notes—The scaly cap, large double ring and the somewhat bulbous base distinguishes this from the other *Agaricus* species. It is probably edible for most people, but it should be tried with caution at first. In some persons it causes a mild gastric disturbance.

Agaricus meleagris (placomyces)

59. Agaricus silvaticus
Woodland agaric; edible with caution. Spores purple-brown.

Cap—1-1/2 to 5 inches wide. Ovate then convex, becoming broadly convex with age; dry. White, covered with densely arranged pinkish brown, somewhat hairy scales, often turning a reddish tinge where bruised or cut. Margin slightly inrolled, becoming elevated.
Gills—Free, thin, crowded, rounded at the stem. At first whitish pink, becoming dark reddish or chocolate brown with age.
Flesh—Thick, firm, whitish, slowly bruising reddish brown or turning with age.
Stem—2-1/4 to 5-1/2 inches long, 1/4 to 1/2 inch thick. Dry, usually with an enlarged, almost bulbous base. Whitish, turning dingy pink to brown with age.
Annulus—Persistent, cottony beneath with raised buff patches. Whitish, becoming dingy.
Volva—None.
Odor—Not distinctive.
Taste—Pleasant.
Habitat—Singly or in groups, sometimes clustered on the ground in coniferous and mixed woods from July to October.
Notes—Probably edible to most people, although it causes mild gastric disturbances in some. A similar species, *A. silvicola*, is occasionally found that is pure white, without colored scales; it stains yellow when bruised and has a double annulus. The same precautions should be taken for it as for *A. silvaticus*.

Agaricus silvaticus

GENUS NAEMATOLOMA

This is a rather small genus with purple-brown to dull cinnamon spores. Most caps are rather brightly colored and may or may not be viscid. The gills are adnexed to adnate or subdecurrent. The stems vary from thick and fleshy to fibrous and tough, or slender and cartilaginous. A veil, inconspicuously attached to the margin of the cap, may be present in some species. Many species are small and of little value as food, and one species is reported as poisonous.

60. Naematoloma capnoides
Smoky-gilled woodlover; edible. Spores purple-brown.

Cap—1/2 to 2 inches wide. Convex, becoming flattened, sometimes slightly umbonate, firm. Brightly colored orange-reddish or yellowish brown, paler and more yellowish on the margin. Smooth, margin inrolled with small fragments of a veil attached.
Gills—Adnate, close, narrow, moderately broad, whitish to grayish, becoming purple-brown from staining of the spores.
Flesh—Thick, firm, whitish.
Stem—2 to 3 inches long, 1/8 to 3/8 inch thick, equal to slightly enlarged at the base. Yellow above a faint annular zone, rusty brown below. Hollow.
Annulus—A faint zone on the stem.
Volva—None.
Odor—Not distinctive.
Taste—Mild.
Habitat—In clusters of several on the wood of conifers from August to October.
Notes—Edible but not especially good. Mistaken for *N. fasciculare* which is intensely bitter and considered mildly poisonous by many authors.

Naematoloma capnoides

GENUS STROPHARIA

This genus is characterized by purple-brown spores, gills that are attached to the stem, and an annulus that may or may not be present. The caps are usually viscid. Most species are difficult to identify. This genus should be avoided by the amateur mushroom hunter as some are suspected of being poisonous.

61. Stropharia magnivelaris
Edibility unknown. Spores purple-brown._____

Cap—1/2 to 1-1/4 inches wide. Convex, becoming broadly convex in age, slightly umbonate, viscid. Yellowish to brownish.
Gills—Adnate, close, moderately broad, pale grayish becoming purplish brown.
Flesh—Thick, thinner at the margin, whitish to yellowish.
Stem—1 to 3 inches long, 1/8 to 1/4 inch thick, viscid, equal or nearly so, becoming hollow with age, colored like the cap.
Annulus—Delicate to membranous.
Volva—None.
Odor—Unpleasant.
Taste—Disagreeable.
Habitat—Singly or in groups on the ground in mixed woods. Look for it on the dung of moose and other animals from July to October.
Notes—*Stropharia* are not recommended as food. At least two species are known to be poisonous.

Stropharia magnivelaris

GENUS ROZITES (PHOLIOTA)

This genus is characterized by rusty brown or brown spores, dry, orange to tawny-colored caps that appear pallid from the silky coating, stems that are thick and stocky with a prominent and persistent annulus or ring. This genus was removed from *Pholiota* because of the rudimentary volva and the ring that hangs about midpoint on the stem. *Rozites* (*Pholiota*) *caperata* appears to be the type species for the genus.

62. Rozites (Pholiota) caperata
Gypsy mushroom; edible. Spores brown.

Cap—2 to 6 inches wide. Convex then expanded, fleshy, smooth, sometimes with a thin whitish bloom, more or less uneven or wrinkled. Cinnamon-buff to ochraceous buff color, paler on the margin.
Gills—Adnate, broad, close, sometimes marked with light and dark bands, pallid to becoming brownish with age.
Flesh—Thick, white, firm.
Stem—2-1/2 to 6 inches long, 1/4 to 3/4 inch thick, equal, solid, whitish, smooth, sometimes scurfy with minute white scales at the top above the ring.
Annulus—Large, membranous, remote from the top, always about the midpoint on the stem.
Volva—Usually not evident but sometimes leaving a few traces at the base of the stem, delicate and filmy, whitish to yellowish in color.
Odor—Mild.
Taste—Pleasant.
Habitat—Singly or scattered on the ground in mixed woods from July to October.
Notes—A large colorful mushroom. The stems are tough and should be discarded.

Rozites (Pholiota) caperata

GENUS COPRINUS

The mushrooms of this genus are known as inky caps because the gills and frequently the flesh of the cap dissolve or deliquesce into an inky fluid at maturity. This feature and the black spore color are the distinguishing characteristics of the genus. About 75 species of *Coprini* are found in North America. Many of these are small, delicate fungi and difficult to find or identify. Only a few are used for food, and some of the best known edibles are in this group. The stems are tough and cartilaginous and should be discarded in the field. It is very important that only the very young caps be gathered, and that these be used immediately, because the *Coprini* will dissolve overnight, even in the refrigerator. None of the *Coprinus* genus are known to be poisonous, but one species, *C. atramentarius,* should never be eaten at a meal at which any alcoholic beverage is taken. Taken in combination with alcohol, *Coprinus atramentarius* causes a severe but temporary reaction, which most people get over within a few hours.

63. Coprinus atramentarius
Inky cap; edible with caution. Spores black.———————————

Cap—1 to 3 inches wide. Ovoid, expanding to conic or campanulate. Gray to brownish. Lobed and folded, silky smooth, becoming tattered on the margin with age.
Gills—Free, crowded, broad; at first white, becoming black and dissolving into an inky fluid.
Flesh—Thin, delicate, brownish gray to off-white.
Stem—2 to 6 inches long, 1/4 to 3/4 inch thick, equal or narrowing at the base, smooth, hollow.
Annulus—Usually at the base, soon vanishing.
Volva—None.
Odor—Pleasant.
Taste—Mild.
Habitat—Usually in clusters on the ground in association with buried wood from July to September.
Notes—If alcohol is taken with a meal in which *C. atramentarius* is eaten, a severe but temporary reaction usually follows, consisting of profuse sweating, flushed face, heart palpitations and cold hands and feet. Recovery is usually within a few hours.

Coprinus atramentarius

64. Coprinus comatus
Shaggy mane, lawyer's wig; edible. Spores black.

Cap—2 to 6 inches long, 1 to 2-1/2 inches thick, cylindrical or barrel-shaped, gradually expanding and becoming somewhat bell-shaped. Brownish covering that breaks up into shaggy scales exposing the whitish flesh. Margin split and recurved outward.
Gills—Nearly free, crowded, broad. White turning pink then black and gradually dissolving into an inky fluid starting at the margin of the cap upward.
Flesh—Thin, soft and fragile.
Stem—2 to 6 inches long, 1/4 to 3/4 inch thick, equal or tapering upward, slightly bulbous at the base, smooth, hollow.
Annulus—Movable, usually at the base, thin, whitish.
Volva—None.
Odor—Mild.
Taste—Mild.
Habitat—Along roadsides and in fields, old meadows and clearings, singly but mostly in groups. More common in the fall, but may be found from June through October, or later if the season is mild.
Notes—One of the "foolproof four" of C. M. Christensen. There's no mistaking this mushroom for any other species. The young shaggy manes are a delight to eat—they have a superb flavor all their own. Use them immediately, because the fresh mushrooms will mature and dissolve overnight, even in the refrigerator. Discard the stems as they are tough and stringy.

Coprinus comatus 163

65. Coprinus micaceus
Shining inky cap; edible. Spores black.───────────────

Cap—1/2 to 2 inches wide. Ovate to elliptical, becoming conic to campanulate. Tan to ochraceous brown, fading to whitish with age, and covered with minute glistening particles that may disappear in older specimens. Strongly striated, smooth on the disk, more or less lobed on the margin.
Gills—Adnate, crowded, broad, whitish turning purplish to black with age, and dissolving into an inky fluid.
Flesh—Thin, soft, whitish.
Stem—1 to 3 inches long, 1/8 to 1/4 inch thick, equal, silky, white, hollow.
Annulus—None.
Volva—None.
Odor—Not distinctive.
Taste—Not distinctive.
Habitat—In dense clusters on the ground around old stumps and buried wood from July to October.
Notes—May appear over and over after a rain, and for many years where a tree or old stump was removed.

Coprinus micaceus 165

GENUS GOMPHIDIUS

This is a small genus characterized by their blackish spores, decurrent waxy distant gills, and caps that are usually more or less slimy-viscid with a viscid veil that leaves a trace of a ring and causes the stem to be viscid also. They are not attractive as food because of the slimy coating and the watery flesh, but they have a striking and unusual appearance.

66. Gomphidius glutinosus
Edible. Spores black. _____

Cap—2 to 4 inches wide. Convex, becoming flattened and often depressed; smooth, viscid to glutinous. Livid purplish brown. Often with remains of a viscid veil.
Gills—Decurrent, forked, distant, waxy; at first whitish, turning smoky gray to blackish.
Flesh—White, unchanging when bruised, sometimes pinkish with age.
Stem—1-1/2 to 3-1/2 inches long, 1/4 to 3/4 inch thick, equal or tapering to the base, smooth. Whitish to pale brownish, yellow at the base. Sheathed by a viscid veil that leaves an annular line near the top.
Annulus—Inconspicuous or absent, appears as an annular line on the stem.
Volva—None.
Odor—Not distinctive.
Taste—Mild to slightly acid.
Habitat—Singly or in groups on the ground of coniferous woods from August to September.
Notes—Generally considered inedible because of the very viscid to slimy caps and stems, but most authors consider this mushroom nonpoisonous, if a bit distasteful.

Gomphidius glutinosus 167

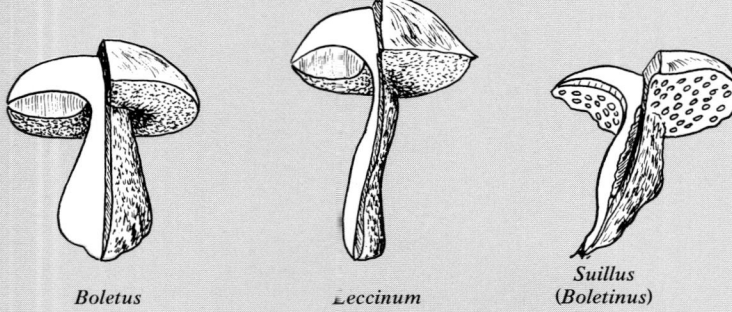

Figure 7—Fleshy Pore Fungi

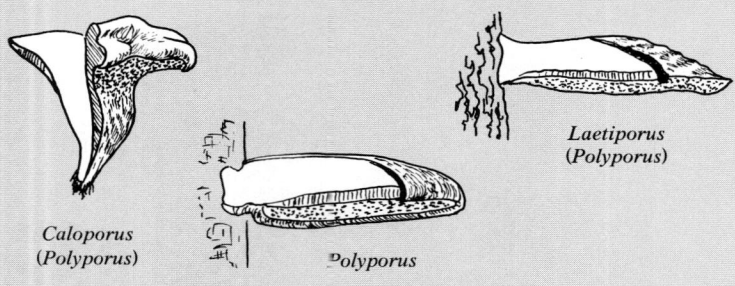

Figure 8—Woody Pore Fungi

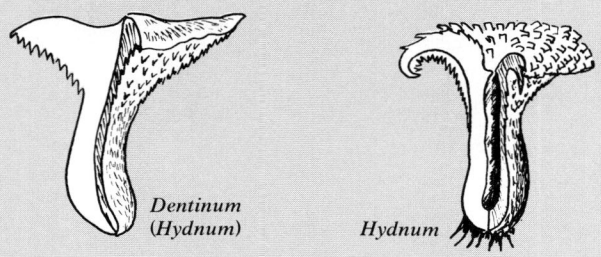

Figure 9—Toothed, or Hedgehog, Fungi

Chapter 7
Mushrooms Without Gills

This chapter includes descriptions of 35 species of mushrooms without gills (color plate numbers 67 through 101) representing 21 genera of the following 8 families:

Boletaceae   *Helvellaceae*
Polyporaceae   *Lycoperdaceae*
Hydnaceae   *Pezizaceae*
Clavariaceae   *Geoglossaceae*

Cross sections of typical mushrooms are shown in Figures 7 through 14, on pages 168 and 171.

To be sure of identifying mushrooms correctly, use the keys given in Chapter 4.

The pore fungi are mushrooms with small, tubelike pores. There are two families. The fleshy pore fungi (family *Boletaceae;* see Figure 7) have caps much like the gilled mushrooms. Most of the woody pore fungi (family *Polyporaceae;* see Figure 8) have caps shaped like shelves or brackets extending outward from trees, stumps and logs. Instead of gills they all have an undercovering of closely packed tubes or pores in which the spores are formed and dropped at maturity. Many of these mushrooms are edible; some are inedible because of certain characteristics, and some are considered poisonous, or at least sickeners.

The toothed, or hedgehog, fungi (family *Hydnaceae;* see Figure 9) are unique and unmistakable: They have toothlike spines. Most are edible, or become inedible only through the infestation of insects. Some have caps like the gill fungi, but instead of gills have a series of spinelike teeth hanging down underneath. These are sometimes called the hedgehog fungi because of the spiny look to the teeth. Some of the toothed fungi grow in a great mass on rotting logs, stumps and trees.

The club, or coral, fungi (family *Clavariaceae;* see Figure 10) bear their spores on stalks of corallike growths These mostly edible mushrooms appear as variously colored vegetable material growing upright on the ground, and on logs, stumps and trees.

The sac, or sponge, fungi (family *Helvellaceae;* see Figure 11) bear their spores in sacs on spongelike bodies. Most of them have a wrinkled convolute cap with a pitted, honeycombed exterior in which the spores are held until maturity. The sponge mushrooms are usually the earliest to appear each spring, and are some of the most sought-after species; many collectors concentrate on just these. Because some are poisonous, or at least considered dangerous, identification is very important.

The puffballs, or stomach fungi (family *Lycoperdaceae;* see Figure 12), are unmistakable once you learn their characteristics. Most are edible, but become unpalatable or inedible with age.

You should always cut a puffball lengthwise to be sure that you are not getting a button stage of the poisonous amanita mushroom. The puffball will be homogeneously solid white inside, and show no evidence of rudimentary gills, cap and stem (see Figure 3, page 5).

Puffballs are covered with an outer skin or rind which encloses the spore-forming cells within. When young they are very good to eat, but as they mature they turn yellow, then brown from the spore color, and become infested with the larvae of insects.

The cup fungi (family *Pezizaceae* see Figure 13) are usually brightly colored, yellowish through dark brown, cuplike growths with thin, brittle flesh. They grow on the ground in poor soils or on rotting wood.

The earth tongues (family *Geoglossaceae;* see Figure 14) are small, upright mushrooms shaped like spatulas or flattened clubs. They are solitary. Most species are dark-colored, but some are light brown or green to yellowish. They grow on the ground in leaf mold and forest humus.

FLESHY PORE FUNGI, FAMILY BOLETACEAE

This family of mushrooms comprises species that have the stature and shape of the gilled fungi, and are soft and fleshy, but bear their spores in tubes or pores rather than on lamellae or gills. The flesh of some caps and stems changes color when cut or bruised, and a few species with this characteristic are considered poisonous. The pores or tubes underneath the caps also vary in color from whitish to a dark red, almost blood-red. Those having the red pore mouths should be avoided. The boletes become infested with insect larvae quite early, but if collected during the button stage of their development are usually firm and unaffected by insects. The tubes of mature specimens should be discarded as they tend to become quite slimy when they are cooked. Some of the best edible mushrooms are found in this group, and every collector should be aware of them.

 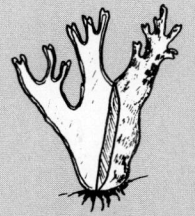 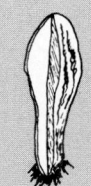

Ramaria (*Clavaria*)   *Clavicorona* (*Clavaria*)   *Clavariadelphus*

Figure 10—Club, or Coral, Fungi

  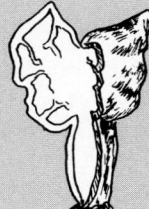 

Morchella   *Verpa*   *Helvella*   *Gyromitra* (*Helvella*)

Figure 11—Sac, or Sponge, Fungi

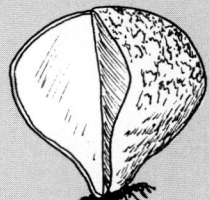 

Calvatia   *Lycoperdon*

Figure 12—Puffballs, or Stomach Fungi

 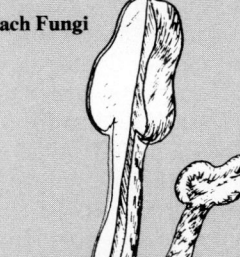

Peziza and Aleuria   *Spathularia*

Figure 13—Cup Fungi   **Figure 14—Earth Tongues**

67. Boletus edulis
King bolete, cep, steinpilz; edible Spores olive-brown._____

Cap—2 to 8 inches or more wide. Hemispherical, convex, becoming expanded to a pincushion shape, occasionally depressed and irregular in form. Margin incurved, later expanded and sometimes very uneven. Surface color varies, but is usually some shade of brown. The surface may be slightly rough or velvety to the touch. The cap is slightly viscid in damp air.

Pores—Small, roundish and regular; whitish, turning yellowish then greenish yellow.

Tubes—Long and thin, round toward the stem and free of it, white or dingy, turning yellowish or greenish yellow in age, easily detached from the cap.

Flesh—Firm; whitish, except immediately under the cuticle it is brownish, does not change color on contact with air or with bruising.

Stem—2 to 6 inches long, 1 to 2 inches thick. Becoming pear-shaped, always thick and solid. White to light hazel, lighter toward the base. Covered more or less with a network of reticulations starting from the top downward, lighter than the stem, turning darker and often quite faint. The stem is hard, stuffed, becoming spongy and fibrous with age.

Odor—Pleasant and mild.

Taste—Pleasant and mild.

Habitat—On the ground, singly or in groups in mixed woods, particularly in open places and on the edge of forests from July to October.

Notes—One of the most desirable of the boletes and highly prized any place in the world where it can be gathered. It may be cooked or used in many ways: fried, boiled, baked broiled, dried, frozen or preserved in oil. Pick the large firm young buttons, which are sometimes as large as a baseball. Consistency is like that of a raw potato and the flavor is excellent.

Boletus edulis 173

68. Boletus erythropus
Edible. Spores olive-brown.───────────────────

Cap—2 to 7 inches in diameter. Convex. Varying in color from almost rufous with an olive tinge to brown. Minutely hairy, dry. Margin inrolled, becoming expanded, somewhat wavy and irregular.
Pores—Reddish, turns blue when bruised.
Tubes—Long, thin, yellow-green.
Flesh—Solid, yellowish, turning blue when cut or bruised.
Stem—2 to 6 inches long, 1/2 to 1-1/2 inches thick. Shape varies, mostly pearlike or tapering at the base. Yellowish color obscured by reddish stippling. No network or reticulations.
Odor—Mild.
Taste—Pleasant.
Habitat—Singly or in groups on the ground of mixed woods on poor soils from July to October.
Notes—Although listed as an edible species, it has two strikes against it: the red pore mouths and the habit of turning blue when bruised or cut. It should be tried with caution when first eating it. Cook as any of the boletes. Discard the tubes as they become slimy when cooked.

69. Boletus mirabilis
Edible. Spores olive-brown.

Cap—2 to 5 inches in diameter. Convex, densely woolly to hairy, dry. Dark reddish brown color.
Pores—Angular, small, yellowish.
Tubes—Long, depressed at the stem, sulphur yellow, becoming mustard yellow in age.
Flesh—Lemon yellow, sometimes turning reddish when cut or bruised.
Stem—5 to 10 inches long, 1 to 2 inches thick, club-shaped to bulbous, widest near the base. Variable large whitish reticulations or network at the top and sometimes covering the whole stem, often disappearing. Whitish near the base only.
Odor—Pleasant and mild.
Taste—Pleasant and mild.
Habitat—Solitary or in groups on rotting conifer logs and stumps, July to October.
Notes—This mushroom is sometimes attacked by a parasitic white mold which renders it inedible. This species does not become infested with insect larvae as readily as the other boletes. Collected when young and firm and not parasitized, it makes a desirable food species. Cook as any of the fleshy pore mushrooms.

Boletus mirabilis

70. Leccinum aurantiacum
Orange bolete; edible. Spores olive-brown._____

Cap—1-1/2 to 6 inches in diameter. Convex. Orange-yellow to reddish orange to reddish brown. Dry, minutely hairy, rarely smooth, margin irregular and having fragments of a veil attached.
Pores—Close, small, round, whitish to cream color turning grayish.
Tubes—Adnate to adnexed, mostly free; dingy white to creamy to gray, long and thin.
Flesh—Firm, whitish to pinkish, turning slightly blue when cut or bruised, finally becoming grayish to blackish.
Stem—2 to 6 inches long, 1/2 to 2 inches thick, tapering upward or nearly equal, more or less scaly, the projections becoming reddish brown, finally blackish, solid, sometimes turning a bluish color at the base when cut.
Odor—Pleasant.
Taste—Pleasant.
Habitat—Singly or in groups on the ground in deciduous woods, usually around birch and poplar (cottonwood) from July to October.
Notes—One of our commonest boletes and easy to recognize with its orange cap and appendiculate margin. Collect the buttons for firm, potatolike specimens and cook as you would any of the edible boletes.

Leccinum aurantiacum

71. Leccinum scabrum
Rough stemmed bolete; edible. Spores olive-brown.———————

Cap—2 to 5 inches in diameter. Convex, becoming plane, velvety to smooth, slightly viscid when wet. Color varies from pallid to tawny-brown, grayish brown or blackish brown. Margin slightly inrolled to becoming elevated in age.
Pores—Very small, round, yellowish white, turning grayish.
Tubes—Long and thin, rounded toward the stem, free, dingy white turning grayish, soft.
Flesh—Soft, whitish turning pink then reddish and slightly violet when exposed to the air, later grayish and finally blackish, turning blue when cut or bruised, then blackish.
Stem—3 to 5 inches long, 1/2 to 3/4 inch thick, tapering upward to nearly equal, with whitish to grayish to blackish scabrous dots, solid, turning blue at the base when cut or bruised.
Odor—Pleasant.
Taste—Pleasant.
Habitat—Singly or in groups on the ground in open woods or meadows from July to October.
Notes—Even dried it turns blackish. It does not keep well and should be used as soon as possible after picking. Cook as you would any edible bolete, discarding the tubes as they tend to get slimy when cooked. It has a good flavor but an unappetizing appearance because it turns black while it's cooking.

72. Leccinum insigne
Orange bolete; edible. Spores olive-brown.

Cap—3 to 8 inches in diameter. Convex to broadly rounded at maturity. Color is always some shade of orange. Somewhat viscid, slightly velvety to the touch, slightly sticky or dry, sometimes cracked in dry weather.
Pores—Small, round, whitish becoming dingy brownish and tinted olive in age.
Tubes—Long, thin, soft, whitish, becoming dingy tan, easily separated from the flesh of the cap and each other.
Flesh—Thick, firm, becoming soft and spongy at maturity, whitish, turning purplish and slate gray, becoming nearly purple-black when cut or bruised.
Stem—5 to 8 inches long, 1 to 1-1/2 inches thick. Broad at the base, tapering upward. Covered with brownish to blackish scales, becoming separated into darkly tipped, rough scales against a whitish background, and becoming purplish black when cut or bruised. Firm and solid early, soft and fibrous in age.
Odor—Mild.
Taste—Mild.
Habitat—Singly or in groups scattered on the ground and along cutbanks in sandy or gravelly soils in July and August, sometimes into October in in milder seasons.
Notes—Very similar to *L. aurantiacum* and *L. scabrum,* differing mainly in the color of the cap and the size of the fruiting body. The buttons are large and firm, have the consistency of a raw potato and cook very well with a good flavor. They turn black when cooking, which may be unpalatable to some.

Leccinum insigne

73. Suillus (Boletinus) cavipes
Edible. Spores brown.───────────────────────

Cap—2 to 4 inches in diameter. Onion-shaped and umbonate, becoming convex and expanded. Brown to golden yellow or violaceous brown, sometimes light to dark hazel. Feels like suede. Margin wavy and often lobed, sometimes elevated, occasionally the remains of a veil at its edge.
Pores—Large, angular, arranged in arcs from the stem to the margin, pale yellow, becoming olive-yellow with age.
Tubes—Short and decurrent, pale yellow, becoming a light greenish yellow, not easily detached from the cap.
Flesh—Firm, pale yellowish, no color change on exposure to air.
Stem—1 to 3 inches long, 1/4 to 1/2 inch thick, swollen at the midpoint, more or less reticulated above the annulus, yellow above, brownish below, soon hollow.
Annulus—Delicate, whitish, disappearing, sometimes adhering to the margin of the cap.
Odor—None.
Taste—Mild and pleasant.
Habitat—Singly or in groups on the ground of damp woods and swampy places in August to September, and perhaps later.
Notes—The velvety cap with large angular pores and the delicate annulus on the hollow stem or adhering to the cap margin are distinctive. Quite good when young, tends to be tough when mature. It may be dried and used later in soups and gravies.

Suillus (Boletinus) cavipes

WOODY PORE FUNGI, FAMILY POLYPORACEAE

This family of mushrooms is similar to the boletes, but the fruiting bodies are generally woody hard, tough or leathery to corky in consistency. They are almost always found growing on wood. Because of their tough consistency they are of limited interest for food, but a few species are edible when young and fresh. Typically, they appear as shelf or bracketlike growths on live and dead trees, stumps and logs. One polypore, *Laetiporus (Polyporus) sulphureus,* the sulphur shelf or chicken of the woods, is very common in Alaska and considered one of the better eating of the group.

74. Caloporus (Polyporus) ovinus (Albatrellus ovinus, Scutiger ovinus)
Sheep polypore; edible. Spores white.

Cap—1-1/2 to 5 inches in diameter. Whitish becoming yellowish to tan in age. Convex, becoming expanded, cuticle smooth, becoming split into rectangular patches against a lighter background with age, margin wavy or undulated to lobed.
Pores—Small, round, whitish turning lemon yellow.
Tubes—Short, decurrent, white, turning lemon yellow.
Flesh—Firm but fragile, white, turning lemon yellow.
Stem—1 to 3 inches long, 1/4 to 3/4 inch thick, central to excentric, white, thickest at the top, tapering somewhat at the base, sometimes clustered from a common point of attachment.
Odor—Pleasant.
Taste—Almondlike.
Habitat—Singly or in groups or clusters on the ground of coniferous woods from July to October in milder seasons.
Notes—Good as long as the mushroom is young. Discard the tough stem. The mushroom should be boiled first to tenderize it before normal cooking. It may be served raw, cut up, and seasoned with oil, salt and pepper.
New generic classifications have placed these mushrooms into all four genera, but *Caloporus* seems to be the most popular and better known.

Caloporus (Polyporus) ovinus

75. Laetiporus (Polyporus) sulphureus
Sulphur shelf, chicken of the woods; edible. Spores white._____

Cap—Fruiting body a massive cluster of overlapping, more or less horizontal, shelflike growths 12 to 18 inches across, and often extending outward for 12 inches or more. Bright sulphur yellow to yellow-orange, sessile, upper surface smooth, if somewhat uneven, margin thick, wavy to undulate, lobed.
Pores—Small, rounded, sulphur yellow.
Tubes—Short, yellow, extends from one cap connection to another.
Flesh—Thick, soft as cheese, juicy, exuding amber drops. Yellowish. As the fungus matures, the flesh becomes hard, tough, woody, dry and light.
Stem—Absent or sessile, a whitish base turning yellowish.
Odor—Pleasant.
Taste—Somewhat acidy.
Habitat—In clusters on living and dead trees and old stumps and logs of mixed woods from July to September.
Notes—One of the "foolproof four" of C. M. Christensen. There's no mistaking this for any other species. When young it is eminently edible. Use just the outer margin of the shelf. Delicious fried in butter or vegetable oil, and many other ways in which it is prepared.

Laetiporus (Polyporus) sulphureus

76. Polyporus (Piptoporus) betulinus
Birch polypore; edibility unknown, but questionable.
Spores probably white to yellowish._____

Cap—1-1/4 to 10 inches long, 1-1/4 to 6 inches wide. Elongated to circular, convex, attached by a lateral stemlike umbo or knob, sessile; whitish early, turning yellowish buff with age; smooth, somewhat scurfy; thick, sterile inrolled margin projects below the tube surface.
Pores—Small, round, white.
Tubes—Short, close, rigid and easily separated from the cap.
Flesh—Elastic and springy, becoming corky when dry, whitish.
Stem—Absent or very short, mostly sessile.
Odor—Mild.
Taste—Somewhat bitterish.
Habitat—On living or dead birch trees, stumps and logs from June to October.
Notes—The young specimens may be fit to eat if you don't mind the bitter taste. Most authors list this species as inedible, or an unknown. A very showy fungus and commonly found wherever birch trees grow.

Polyporus (Piptoporus) betulinus

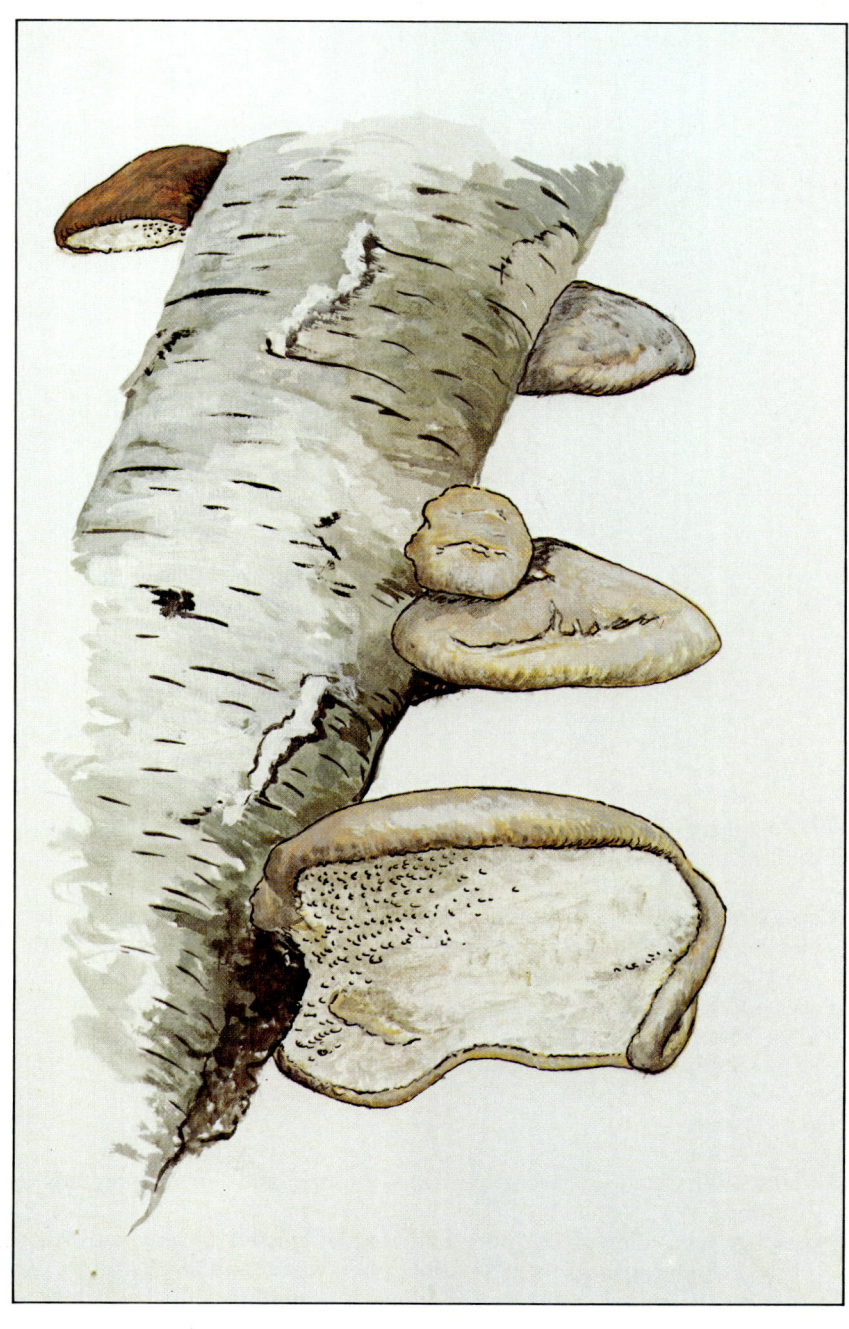

77. Polyporus (Polystictus) versicolor
Edibility unknown. Spores white.───────────────

Cap—Fruiting body 1 to 3 inches wide. Occurring in overlapping clusters, leathery, colorfully zoned from whitish, yellow, to red and green, velvety to the touch, frequently a hairy surface.
Pores—Very small, white.
Tubes—Short, close, rigid.
Flesh—Thin, tough, leathery when young, corky when old.
Stem—Absent or sessile.
Odor—None.
Taste—None.
Habitat—On dead or decaying trees, stumps and logs from July to October.
Notes—A very colorful polypore and seldom missed by any mushroom hunter. Some authors list it as edible when young and fresh, but its very tough and leathery consistency makes it a doubtful food mushroom.

Polyporus (Polystictus) versicolor 193

TOOTHED, OR HEDGEHOG, FUNGI, FAMILY HYDNACEAE

The *Hydnaceae* are a large group of fungi in which the spores are borne on the surface of spinelike teeth developing from the underside of the fruiting body. The fruiting body varies in shape from a simple layer of tissuelike structures on wood, to large shelf or bracketlike forms and branched structures, or to a mushroomlike body with a cap and stem. Most *Hydnaceae* grow on wood, but many are found on the ground. Most are tough, fibrous and somewhat woody and as such are not edible. A few species are good food mushrooms. None of the *Hydnaceae* are known to be poisonous.

78. Dentinum (Hydnum) repandum

Spreading hedgehog; edible. Spores white._____

Cap—2 to 6 inches wide. Convex, becoming somewhat flattened, sometimes depressed, margin uneven and irregular, whitish to buff color, dry, smooth, minutely velvety.
Teeth—Slightly decurrent, fleshy, soft, mostly round, medium long, whitish to cream-colored.
Flesh—Thick, soft, white.
Stem—1/2 to 3 inches long, 1/4 to 1 inch thick, central to excentric, smooth, whitish buff, solid.
Odor—Pleasant.
Taste—Acidy and rather bitter in old specimens.
Habitat—Singly or in groups, rings and rows on the ground of mixed woods from July to October.
Notes—Seldom infested with insect larvae when young. Older mushrooms should be boiled and the water discarded to get rid of the bitter taste. When collecting this desirable, edible species, the stem should be left in the ground to assure future growths of mushrooms.

Dentinum (Hydnum) repandum

79. Hericium laciniatum
Edible. Spores colorless, white in mass._____

Cap—A large fruiting body consisting of an intricate system of fleshy branches up to 10 to 12 inches across, with whitish teeth on the underside of the branches.
Teeth—1/4 to 1/2 inch long, cylindric spines, more or less in tufts, whitish to pale cream color.
Flesh—Fibrous, white.
Stem—Stout, thick, whitish, sometimes appearing absent.
Odor—Mild.
Taste—Mild.
Habitat—On logs and stumps of trees in mixed woods in August and September.
Notes—Very similar to *Hydnum coralloides* except the teeth are shorter and the fruiting body is more branched. A good find for the mushroom hunter as these are eminently edible, and one fresh fruiting body should make a meal.

Hericium laciniatum

80. Hydnum imbricatum
Brick top or scaly hydnum; edible. Spores brownish._____

Cap—2-1/2 to 8 inches and sometimes wider. Convex with a central depression, then flattened and becoming almost funnel-shaped with age. Light hazel-gray color covered with large brown scales, turning darker brown with age. Scales are arranged in concentric circles and grow thicker and coarser toward the center of the cap. Margin often incurled and then elevating with scales disappearing along outer edge as the mushroom ages.
Teeth—Stiff, close, regular, decurrent along the stem, fragile, ashy gray becoming bluish gray in color.
Flesh—Firm, whitish, turning grayish.
Stem—Stout and squat, 1-1/2 to 4-1/2 inches long, 1/2 to 1-1/2 inches thick, rounded at the base, hollow. Yellowish, turning ashy gray.
Odor—Slight.
Taste—Mild to slightly bitter.
Habitat—Singly or in groups, rows or semicircles on the ground in mixed, but usually coniferous, woods from August to October.
Notes—Mistaken for a closely related species, *Hydnum fennicum* (*scabrosum*) which is very bitter tasting. Always boil the mushrooms and discard the water to get rid of the bitter taste in mature specimens.

Hydnum imbricatum 199

81. Hydnum fennicum
Bitter hydnum; edibility questionable—edible but bitter.
Spores brownish.──────────────────────────

Cap—2 to 8 inches wide or wider. Convex to flattened with a depressed center. Surface dark brown to reddish-purplish brown and covered with thick brown scales arranged concentrically, becoming thin and sparse toward the margin. Margin uneven, wavy to lobed.
Teeth—Slender, firm, decurrent along the stem, dark umber at the base, to whitish tips, some shorter teeth scattered among those of regular length.
Flesh—Fibrous, brittle, light buff-brown.
Stem—1 to 4 inches long, 1/4 to 1 inch thick, rounded at the base, same color as the cap, becoming darker at the base which has blue flesh.
Odor—Not distinctive.
Taste—Very bitter.
Habitat—Singly or in groups, rows or semicircles in mixed woods, usually coniferous, from August to October.
Notes—Much like *Sarcodon (Hydnum) imbricatum* but differs in the bluish flesh at the base of the stem, more slender teeth and the very bitter taste. Sometimes this bitterness may be removed by boiling the fungus and discarding the water.

Hydnum fennicum

CLUB, OR CORAL, FUNGI, FAMILY CLAVARIACEAE

This family of mushrooms consists of forms with erect, simple or branched fruiting bodies having no teeth, pores or gills. The entire fruiting body surface is spore-bearing. It resembles coral formations growing on rotting wood, but sometimes occurs on the ground. The coloration will vary from almost white or yellow to reddish or violet in some species. Most of the group are considered edible, but one species, *Ramaria formosa*, is considered poisonous. Many are tough or bitter or otherwise unpleasant to the taste. The *Clavariaceae* are unmistakable and easily found by the amateur mushroom hunter, but the differentiation into species is a little more difficult, and some care should be taken if these are collected for food.

82. Ramaria (Clavaria) rufescens
Edible. Spores yellow-brown._____

Fruiting Body—2 to 4 inches high, much branched. Pinkish to violet, sometimes lavender. Erect, having a cauliflowerlike appearance.
Stem—Short, thick, 1/2 to 1 inch in diameter, tapering downward, dingy pink to pale violaceous.
Odor—Mild.
Taste—Mild.
Habitat—On the ground as single clumps or in groups, sometimes in rows along a buried root, in mixed woods from July to October.
Notes—Similar to *Ramaria botrytis* except for the overall coloration. *R. botrytis* is whitish cream, with pink to rosy tips to the branches. It is also edible.

83. Ramaria (Clavaria) flava
Golden coral; edible. Spores yellow-buff._____

Fruiting Body—2 to 6 inches high. Many-branched, main branches arising from a short, thick, whitish base. Erect. Bright yellow, often becoming brownish with age. Sometimes toothed at the end of the branches.
Stem—A thickening at the base of the fruiting body, round, short and thick, erect, pale yellow to brownish.
Odor—Mild and pleasant.
Taste—Mild and pleasant.
Habitat—On the ground in single clumps or groups of clumps, in a row or semicircle, amid sphagnum of moist woods from July to October.
Notes—There are many yellow clavarias and most are edible except *Ramaria formosa*, not commonly found in Alaska. *Clavaria aurea* and *Ramaria flava* are very similar; the only differences are the pale yellow color of *Ramaria flava* and *Clavaria aurea*'s not turning brown when bruised. Both species are edible.

Ramaria (Clavaria) flava

84. Clavaria cristata
Edible. Spores white to yellowish buff._____

Fruiting Body—2 to 4 inches tall. Whitish to pale gray, or minutely tinged with violet. Branches toothed at their tips, often irregular and flattened.
Stem—1/4 to 1/2 inch thick, round, up to 3/4 inch long, branching into the fruiting body, same color as the plant.
Odor—Mild.
Taste—Mild.
Habitat—On the ground in single tufts to groups of many tufts, mostly coniferous woods, in September and October.
Notes—Harmlessly mistaken for *Ramaria* (*Clavaria*) *rufescens* because of the slight purplish or violet tinge, but the differences are apparent on close examination. Both are edible. *C. cinerea* is similar to *C. cristata* but somewhat larger.

Clavaria cristata 207

85. Clavicorona (Clavaria) pyxidata
Edible. Spores white to yellowish buff.

Fruiting Body—2 to 6 inches high, much branched, branches enlarged upward with toothlike projections at the crown, whitish to pale yellow with age. Tips of branches are like inverted cones crowned with whitish yellowish teeth.
Stem—A sessile base, usually inconspicuous, often becoming dingy brown with age.
Odor—Mild.
Taste—Slightly peppery (acid).
Habitat—Always on wood, mostly deciduous trees, stumps and logs, rarely on conifers, in July and August.
Notes—Collect it when it is young and fresh. When old, it tends to become tough and more peppery tasting.

Clavicorona (Clavaria) pyxidata

86. Clavariadelphus pistillaris
Edible. Spores whitish to buff._____

Fruiting Body—3 to 6 inches high, 1 to 2-1/2 inches thick. Club-shaped, coarsely wrinkled longitudinally. Orange-red to brownish red, tinged yellowish. Becoming hollow in age.
Base—White and finely downy-hairy just over the very lower part.
Flesh—Firm, whitish, becoming hollow with age.
Odor—Not distinctive.
Taste—Bitterish.
Habitat—Occurs singly or in groups on the ground of mixed woods, mostly deciduous trees, in August and into September.
Notes—The bitter taste will disappear upon boiling the mushroom and discarding the water.

Clavariadelphus pistillaris

87. Clavariadelphus sachaliensis
Edibility unknown. Spores ochraceous._____

Fruiting Body—1 to 3 inches high, 1/4 to 1/2 inch thick. Narrowly club-shaped, sometimes flattened, surface rough. Salmon to orange-buff color, with a finely white downy base.
Flesh—Firm, whitish.
Odor—Not distinctive.
Taste—Slightly bitter.
Habitat—In clusters and groups on the ground in coniferous woods in August and September.
Notes—*C. ligula,* usually not found in Alaska, is very similar but has a whitish spore color. Suspect that the young specimens collected would lose the bitter taste with boiling.

Clavariadelphus sachaliensis

88. Clavariadelphus truncatus
Edible. Spores ochraceous.

Fruiting Body—3 to 6 inches high, 1 to 3 inches thick. Club-shaped, often with a flattened crown which sometimes ruptures in age revealing the hollow interior. Bright golden yellow to orange-yellow turning brownish with age. Sometimes very wrinkled or veined near the top, the base smooth with a whitish-hairy covering.
Flesh—Thin, white, hollow at the top.
Odor—Not distinctive.
Taste—Sweetish.
Habitat—Singly to scattered, sometimes in groups of several on the ground of coniferous woods from July to September, sometimes later.
Notes—Closely related to *C. pistillaris* but is more yellow with a broader, more flattened top and is not bitter to the taste.

Clavariadelphus truncatus

SAC, OR SPONGE, FUNGI, FAMILY HELVELLACEAE

The fruiting body of members of this group of fungi are spongelike in appearance, some having a pitted surface, while others appear smooth but convoluted and lobed. Most are of some shade of brown color, from yellowish through olivaceous. Many are edible and desirable to pick for food, but others of the group are dangerous, and some are considered poisonous. You should never eat any of the *Helvellaceae* raw, as even the edible species may cause a severe reaction. Some of this group are the first to appear each spring, often before the snow is completely gone, and have a short growing season of 2 or 3 weeks. Others seem to thrive and grow throughout the regular late spring to fall mushroom season. They all like wet, marshy, wooded places in general, but may be found most anywhere where the conditions are optimum for their growth.

The genus *Morchella*—succulent, eminently edible mushrooms—has some of the most desirable collector species to be found in Southcentral Alaska. For many years, one of the best places to find them has been the Kenai Peninsula throughout the National Moose Range, especially in the area of the big burn near Cooper Landing. Unfortunately, there has been some evidence that mushrooms gathered here have caused some illness that is attributed to their having assimilated fire-retardant chemicals. Be cautious in eating mushrooms from any burned-over area where fire-retardant chemicals have been used.

89. Gyromitra (Helvella) esculenta
Brain mushroom; <u>poisonous</u>   Spores yellowish.

Cap—1 to 3 inches wide. Varies in shape but more or less lobed to very irregular, surface wrinkled and folded or convoluted. As the common name suggests, brainlike in appearance, not pitted. Reddish to dark brown. Fragile.
Stem—3/4 to 2 inches long, 1/2 to 1 inch thick, whitish, fragile, somewhat grooved, hollow, smooth exterior.
Flesh—Fragile to brittle, thin, waxy.
Odor—Not distinctive; mild.
Taste—Faint. Taste, but do not swallow.
Habitat—On the ground in coniferous or mixed woods in the spring, from late May through July, sometimes later. Frequents cool, damp, shady and sandy places, sometimes at the bases of old stumps.
Notes—Some people have eaten this mushroom with impunity, but there have been several deaths attributed to it both in Europe and North America. Contains Group E toxins. Never eat any of the *Helvellaceae* raw.

Gyromitra (Helvella) esculenta

90. Helvella infula
Hooded helvella; <u>poisonous</u>. Spores whitish.————————

Cap—2 to 4 inches thick. Curled and shriveled, irregular, lobed, sometimes erect and often falling over the stem and somewhat saddle-shaped. Upper surface whitish brown in color. Hollow, irregularly chambered, fragile.
Stem—3/4 to 2 inches long, 1/4 to 3/4 inch thick, round, or in the form of an inverted cone, usually covered with longitudinal ridges and grooves, whitish or pale color covered with a whitish down, becoming hollow and often compressed with age.
Flesh—Thin, waxy, fragile.
Odor—Pleasant.
Taste—Pleasant. Taste, but do not swallow.
Habitat—On the ground in damp places of mixed woods, occurs singly or in groups of two or three, sometimes near decaying stumps and logs, in July and August.
Notes—Some people apparently can eat this species with impunity, but others become very ill with but a small bit. Contains Group E toxins. Never eat any of the *Helvellaceae* raw.

Helvella infula 219

91. Helvella lacunosa
Elfin saddle; edible, but dangerous. Spores whitish.───────────

Cap—3/4 to 1-1/2 inches high, 3/4 to 1-1/2 inches wide. Very lobed, wrinkled and twisted, upper surface rough, smoky brown to blackish, lower surface smooth and an ashy color, irregularly chambered, thin-walled, tough.
Stem—3/4 to 1-1/2 inches long, 1/4 to 3/4 inch thick, irregularly round, covered with longitudinal grooves and ridges, ashy color but lighter toward the base, becoming hollow with age, thin-walled, tough.
Flesh—Thin, tough, whitish to ashy gray.
Odor—None.
Taste—None. Taste, but do not swallow.
Habitat—Singly or in groups on the damp ground in moss or grassy places of mixed woods, sometimes near rotting stumps and logs, from July to September.
Notes—A small helvella, and considered edible by many. Be sure to identify this positively from *H. infula,* considered poisonous for most people. The gray to black cap and the very grooved and ridged stem are distinguishing features. Never eat any of the *Helvellaceae* raw.

92. Morchella angusticeps
Conic morel; edible. Spores yellowish _____

Cap—1 to 3 inches long, 1/2 to 1-1/4 inches wide at the base. Elongated to cone-shaped, surface covered with long pits arranged in vertical rows. Yellowish brown within, edges smoky brown to blackish. Hollow and empty, a grooved attachment to the stem, and not separated from it.
Stem—3/4 to 2-1/2 inches long, 1/2 to 1 inch thick, whitish to yellowish, round, and often enlarged and furrowed at the base, mealy, hollow, inner cap and stem whitish.
Flesh—Waxy, whitish becoming darker, flesh of stem off-white and dingy.
Odor—Mild.
Taste—Pleasant. Taste, but do not swallow.
Habitat—Singly or mostly in groups on the ground in open places of mixed woods. Commonly found in old burned-over woods, especially conifers. Sometimes in large groups on well-drained sandy soils of hillsides in spring, late May and June.
Notes—One of C. M. Christensen's "foolproof four." There's no mistaking this mushroom for any other except by dire carelessness. Similar to *Verpa bohemica* which usually occurs earlier in the season, but which is readily differentiated upon comparison. Never eat any of the *Helvellaceae* raw.

Morchella angusticeps

93. Morchella esculenta
Sponge morel; edible. Spores yellowish.——————————————

Cap—1-1/2 to 2-1/2 inches in diameter. Globose, almost round, surface covered with pits of various shapes and in no order, framed by irregular ridges following the pits. Pits are mostly ocher, the ribs yellowish, giving the cap an all over pale ocher color. Inside hollow and empty, inner wall whitish.
Stem—1-1/2 to 3 inches long, 3/4 to 1-1/2 inches thick, round, much larger at the base, wrinkled, grooved longitudinally, covered with small scurfy tufts just beneath the cap, whitish, becoming ochraceous in age, fragile, hollow.
Flesh—Fragile, waxy, thin, whitish.
Odor—Slight.
Taste—Pleasant. Taste, but do not swallow.
Habitat—Singly or in groups on the ground of mixed open woods, pastures and hillsides on sandy ground, sometimes in rows or semirings. Frequently found in old burned-over woods in spring, late May and June.
Notes—One of C. M. Christensen's "foolproof four." Not mistaken for any other species except in carelessness. Never eat any of the *Helvellaceae* raw.

Morchella esculenta

94. Verpa bohemica
False morel; inedible for some persons. Spores pale yellow._____

Cap—1/2 to 1-1/2 inches long, 1/4 to 1-1/4 inches wide. Somewhat bell-shaped, attached to the stem only at the apex and hanging down around it, margin free from the stem. Yellowish to reddish brown. Has a prominently ridged surface with reticulations.
Stem—1 to 5 inches long, 1/4 to 1 inch thick, round, becoming compressed or flattened, whitish becoming yellowish in age, smooth, cottony at the base, stuffed, becoming hollow when old.
Flesh—Thin, fragile.
Odor—Not distinctive.
Taste—Not distinctive. Taste, but do not swallow.
Habitat—Singly or in groups on the ground of mixed woods, in damp open places, and along stream banks and in rich leaf mold in spring, late May or June, usually before the true morels appear.
Notes—Some authors list this species as edible, and it may be for some people. Others react to it somewhat violently, and if eaten for the first time caution should be exercised. Similar to *Morchella angusticeps* in appearance, but it is easily differentiated by its cap free from the stem. Never eat any *Helvellaceae* raw.

Verpa bohemica

Without Gills

PUFFBALLS, OR STOMACH FUNGI, FAMILY LYCOPERDACEAE
　　The fruiting bodies of most puffballs are usually globular in shape, vary in size from smaller than a golf ball to as large as a basketball. Mostly whitish and turning darker with age, the outer skin is smooth or covered with fragile spines, warts or patches, and breaking apart or opening at the apex at maturity. When young, the interior is homogeneously white with no indication of internal structures resembling a cap, gills or stem. As the puffball ages, the interior turns yellowish, brownish and then dark brown in color, becoming soggy at first, then developing into a dry powder (the spores) which is dispersed into the air. Puffballs are edible when they are young but become bitter and strong-tasting as they mature. (A young one is white inside; yellowing is a sign of age.) To be sure that you are getting a puffball and not the button stage of a poisonous amanita, cut through each puffball from top to bottom; the puffball will lack the rudimentary cap, stem and gill structures that would be found in a button amanita.

95. Calvatia gigantea
Giant puffball; edible. Spores olive-brown.

Fruiting Body—2 to 10 inches, sometimes larger in diameter. A more or less compressed ball attached to the ground by a small pedicel, with a thin rootlike filament growing into the soil. The body is enveloped in a double covering, the outer surface white, becoming hazel-gray color, soft, smooth somewhat velvety and breaking into fragments and falling away in age. Inner covering whitish, becoming yellowish then sooty, thin and fragile, splitting at the top as the fungus matures.
Inner Substance—White and compact, becoming yellow, soft and flabby, then olive-brown and mushy, finally clotted, dry, and tobacco brown in color.
Odor—Good when young, nauseating when old.
Taste—Mild and pleasant when young and fresh.
Habitat—On the ground singly and scattered groups in meadows, fields and pastures from July to September.
Notes—One of C. M. Christensen's "foolproof four" mushrooms.

Calvatia gigantea

96. Lycoperdon perlatum
Gem-studded puffball; edible. Spores olive-brown._____

Fruiting Body—1 to 2-1/2 inches tall, 3/4 to 1-1/2 inches wide. A somewhat inverted pear shape, the outer covering whitish and covered with dense fragile spines surrounded by small warts. As the fungus matures it becomes yellowish to brownish and breaks open at the top emitting the spores. There is no true stem, but a lower peduncle growing into the ground having a short filamentlike root at its base, and is almost always free of any warts and spines, but smooth and whitish in color.
Inner Substance—Flesh white and firm at first, turning yellow and becoming doughy, soggy, and olive color, finally becoming clotted and dusty brown. The inner substance of the lower peduncle is whitish, becoming spongy and tough as it dries with age.
Odor—Mild.
Taste—Pleasant.
Habitat—Singly or in groups, usually several specimens in a clump on the ground in mixed woods, open pastures and fields, and along roadsides. Very common and numerous from July to October.
Notes—One of C. M. Christensen's "foolproof four" mushrooms. It may be eaten raw or cooked in many ways. Harmlessly mistaken for other small puffballs. Puffballs are edible when they are young but become bitter and strong-tasting as they mature. (A young one is white inside; yellowing is a sign of age.) To be sure that you are getting a puffball and not the button stage of a poisonous amanita, cut through each puffball from top to bottom; the puffball will lack the rudimentary cap, stem and gill structures that would be found in a button amanita.

Lycoperdon perlatum 231

97. Lycoperdon pyriforme
Pear-shaped puffball; edible. Spores olive-brown.

Fruiting Body—3/4 to 3 inches high, about 1/2 to 1-1/4 inches wide. Somewhat inverted pear shape tapering downward to a filamentlike root. Outer covering yellowish, covered with darker, almost reddish small warts, falling off in age with the surface then turning smoky yellow with skin dividing into small polygonal, tilelike sections. Opening at the top when old.
Inner Substance—Firm and white when young, turning greenish yellow, yellow-brown and soggy, finally tobacco brown, the dusty spores emerging from the top opening.
Odor—Mild.
Taste—Pleasant.
Habitat—Singly or in groups and clumps of several on rotting stumps and logs, and on sandy ground and grassy places, often in clusters, from July to October.
Notes—Harmlessly mistaken for other small puffballs. Puffballs are edible when they are young but become bitter and strong-tasting as they mature. (A young one is white inside; yellowing is a sign of age.) To be sure that you are getting a puffball and not the button stage of a poisonous amanita, cut through each puffball from top to bottom; the puffball will lack the rudimentary cap, stem and gill structures that would be found in a button amanita.

Lycoperdon pyriforme

CUP FUNGI, FAMILY PEZIZACEAE

Members of this group of specialized fungi appear as thin, fleshy, somewhat brittle, brightly colored, cup-shaped fruiting bodies growing on the ground or on rotting wood. Most are tough or otherwise unpalatable, but a few are known to be edible. The family is easily recognized, but individual species usually require a microscope for exact identification.

98. Peziza badio-confusa
Pig's ears fungus; edible. Spore color unknown._____

Cup—1-1/4 to 4 inches in diameter, shallow. Red-brown to brown. In and out, somewhat wavy or undulate in outline.
Flesh—Thin, brittle.
Stem—Sessile, inconspicuous or absent.
Odor—Not distinctive.
Taste—Not distinctive.
Habitat—Singly or in groups on the ground in mixed woods along roads, cutbanks and trails from July to October.
Notes—Mistaken harmlessly for *P. repanda* which grows on rotten wood. It is also edible.

Peziza badio-confusa 235

99. Peziza repanda
Brownie cup; edible. Spore color unknown.

Cup—2 to 4 inches in diameter. Shallow, cup-shaped, becoming expanded and flattened. Pale brown inside, whitish outside. Smooth, margin even or slightly wavy.
Flesh—Thin, brittle, somewhat waxy.
Stem—Sessile or short stipitate.
Odor—Not distinctive.
Taste—Not distinctive.
Habitat—Singly or in groups on rotting logs and buried wood, occasionally on the ground from July to October.
Notes—Similar to *P. badia,* but differentiated by its habit of growing mostly on wood. None of the *Pezizaceae* are harmful if properly cooked and not aged or spoiled.

Peziza repanda

100. Aleuria (Peziza) aurantia
Orange peel fungus; edible. Spore color unknown.

Cup—1 to 4 inches in diameter. At first a small, hollow, spherelike pinkish globe, becoming cup-shaped as it matures. Inner surface bright orange-red color, outer surface dingy whitish pink. Expanding in age to a shell-like appearance, margin wavy or lobed.
Flesh—Thin, fleshy, fragile, reddish.
Stem—Sessile.
Odor—Pleasant.
Taste—Mild.
Habitat—Single or in groups on the ground in clayish and sandy soils of mixed woods, in grassy spots and along shady roads and trails from August to October.
Notes—May be eaten raw, as in a salad. The bright orange cup is distinctive, but may be mistaken for *Sarcoscypha coccinea,* edibility unknown and uncommon in Alaska, which will have a deep scarlet or red inner cup.

Aleuria (Peziza) aurantia

EARTH TONGUES, FAMILY GEOGLOSSACEAE

This is an unusual group of specialized fungi with a variety of small, variously colored, wrinkled-headed, club-shaped or spatulalike fruiting bodies growing on the ground from leaf mold and mosses. Most are inedible or at least unpalatable, but there are a few species that are known to be edible. Most are small, unobstrusive mushrooms and only the brighter colored specimens are noticed.

101. Spathularia flavida (clavata)
Yellow earth tongue; edible. Spore color unknown.─────────

Cap—1 to 2 inches high, sometimes higher, 1/2 to 1-1/2 inches wide. Horseshoe-shaped, or like a spatula set athwart the stem, smooth, often lobed. Bright to buff-yellow.
Stem—Short, squat, 1 to 2-1/2 inches long, 1/4 to 1/2 inch thick, cylindrical-irregular, distinct from the cap, whitish to yellowish.
Flesh—Cap yellow, stem whitish or yellowish, tough.
Odor—Not distinctive.
Taste—Mildly unpleasant.
Habitat—Singly or in groups, sometimes in rows, on the ground in coniferous woods mostly among moss and needles from August to October.
Notes—Resembles a whitish yellowish cigarette butt topped by a yellow wig, or a coarse yellow spatula with a thick whitish handle.

Spathularia flavida (clavata)

Chapter 8
Mushrooms as Food

Now that you're a mushroom fancier, a full-blown mycophagist if you will, and have used the wild mushrooms you've gathered for your favorite recipes, you will shun the commercial variety, fresh or canned, unless no others are available.

You have probably selected a few choice edible species and experimented with these in your favorite dishes. From the first, you have noticed the difference between the wild and commercial variety in texture and flavor. There is no comparison.

Even *Agaricus campestris,* the meadow mushroom gathered in the wild, is far superior to its cultivated cousin, *Agaricus bisporus* you buy at the market.

Some species of mushrooms may be cooked in their own special way, while others lend themselves well to a great variety of dishes.

MUSHROOMS AND NUTRITION

Mushrooms are a valuable addition to the diet. They offer considerable nutritional value, just as vegetables do. Calories range from 125 to 170 a pound, depending upon the variety. Their protein and trace minerals offer a lot of value for a few calories.

Proteins—Mushrooms have as much protein content as most vegetables (2% to 3%), and 70% to 80% of the protein is digestible.[1]

Vitamins—Wild mushrooms contain many vitamins. They have small amounts of vitamins C and K larger amounts of thiamine (B1), riboflavin (B2), pantothenic acid (B3), and generous amounts of niacin. Some wild varieties contain the forerunner of vitamin D (ergosterol).[2]

Minerals—Like vegetables, mushrooms contain many minerals vital to good health. They are a good source of copper, iron and potassium; they contain small amounts of calcium, phosphorus, magnesium, manganese and sulphur, as well as other trace minerals needed for body function. They are also very low in sodium—an important fact for anyone who is on a low-sodium or low-salt diet.

Amino Acids—These are the building blocks with which the body makes protein (the raw material for your muscles). Mushrooms contain four of the essential amino acids in good quantity, including methionine, a very important sulphur-containing one. For this reason they offer a valuable supplement to the vegetarian diet. A word of warning, however: The protein in mushrooms is not a complete protein and will not sustain growth unless supplemented with other protein sources that fill the lacking essential amino acids.

Different species of mushrooms vary in chemical composition. Average figures show: 88% to 90% water, 4% to 6% carbohydrates, 2% to 3% protein, 1% minerals and only 1% or less fats. These fats are 20% saturated (palmitic), 33% polyunsaturated (linoleic), and 37% mono-unsaturated (oleic).[2, 3, 4]

One pound of cleaned mushrooms, ready to eat, is equivalent in protein to 1-1/2 to 2 ounces of meat (10 to 14 grams). Remember that their content of amino acids is not good enough to replace animal protein, but mushrooms do offer a very good supplement to the diet.

Authorities disagree on the digestibility of mushrooms. Some believe that all the nutrients are fully available, while others [5] believe that none of the carbohydrate is usable and count only the caloric value received from the protein and trace of fat. Probably there is individual variation in how much can be absorbed, depending on the intestinal capacity for digestion of fungi.[6]

1. Rolf Singer, *Mushrooms & Truffles*.
2. Radcliffe F. Robinson, "Food Production by Fungi."
3. *Food Values of Portions Commonly Used, Bowes and Church.*
4. *Composition of Foods.*
5. R. A. McCance and E. M. Widdowson, *Chemical Composition of Foods.*
6. H. A. Harper, *Review of Physiological Chemistry.*

THE PICK OF THE MUSHROOM CROP

Always try to gather the youngest or button stages of the edible gilled and fleshy pore fungi, and the early fresh stages of the other edible fungi which are gathered for the table. Positive identification of mature specimens is very important when you are gathering only the button mushrooms.

Mushrooms should always be "field cleaned"; that is, remove soil, dead leaves and grass as they are gathered. Check mushrooms for insect infestation, discard or cut away infested parts and trim off any animal bites or bruised parts. (Yes, wild animals eat mushrooms.) If there is a lake or stream nearby, it's best to wash the mushrooms before bringing them home. Shake them as dry as possible, especially before putting them into plastic bags.

The stems of some mushrooms tend to be tough and unpalatable, and may be discarded or saved to be used for soups and gravy dishes. In others, such as the fleshy pore fungi, the mature tubes tend to decompose faster than the other parts and may be cut away and left for reseeding.

The fleshy pore fungi and some of the gilled types tend to quickly become infested with insect larvae, usually from the base of the stem upward into the cap area. All insect-infested parts should be cut off and discarded. While I'm sure a little insect protein wouldn't do any harm, it is certainly unpalatable and impairs the mushroom's flavor in cooking.

Some of the more common edible species of mushrooms to be found in Alaska have large button stages and fleshy, firm young stages of growth that are very desirable to the true mycophagist. They are a mushroom gourmet's delight.

The preservation, cooking and eating of mushrooms is not new. Since early times man has collected and eaten many types of wild plants, including mushrooms. Following are methods of preserving mushrooms, tips for using them and specific recipes, including many of my favorites. All are included to provide basic methods for using mushrooms, and the reader is encouraged to experiment and develop his own special ways to cook the edible varieties.

PRESERVING MUSHROOMS

Freezing
Clean and sort mushrooms according to size. Pieces should not be larger than 1 inch across. If freezing in rigid containers, allow 1/2 inch head space; if plastic bags are used, expel excess air from the bag before sealing.

Steam method—To prevent darkening, soak mushrooms for 5 minutes in a solution of 1 pint of water to 1 teaspoon of lemon juice or 1/2 teaspoon of citric acid powder. Drain and steam in covered steamer; 5 minutes for larger pieces and 3-1/2 minutes for smaller ones. Dip in cold water to cool. Drain, pack into containers, seal and freeze at once.

Pan-frying method—Heat mushrooms in butter until almost done (a few minutes only). Cool in air or set pan in cold water. Pack cooled mushrooms into containers, seal and freeze immediately.

Direct method—Mushrooms may be frozen without any processing other than cleaning and sorting. However, mushrooms may become rubbery and less palatable.

Blanching method—Dip small quantities of mushrooms in boiling water; cool immediately by immersing in cold water. Drain, then pack in containers and freeze immediately.

Broiling method—Select large mushrooms, dot with butter and broil until almost done. Cool in air, package with cap side down and freeze immediately.

Drying

Cut large mushrooms in 1/2-inch slices; discard tough stems. Leave small mushrooms whole. Spread mushrooms on sheet pan with layers not more than 1/2 inch deep. Dry in 150° oven (leave oven door open a crack) until mushrooms are leathery dry. Cool mushrooms in air, then pack in plastic bags or foil. Store in cool, dry place.

Pasteurizing dried mushrooms—Preheat oven to 175°. Spread dried mushrooms loosely and not more than 1 inch deep on sheet pan and heat in oven for 10 minutes.

Pureed dried mushrooms—Cook unseasoned cleaned mushrooms, including stems if you wish, by simmering gently for an hour in a small amount of water. Drain and put mushrooms through a food mill, blender or fine sieve to make a puree. Spread puree on a sheet pan, no more than 1/8- to 1/4-inch thick, and dry in sun or in 150° oven (leave oven door open a crack). When thoroughly dry, break into pieces, pasteurize according to directions here, pack in plastic bags, seal securely and store in a cool, dry place. Dried puree may be used in gravy, soup, stew or sauce.

Storing dried mushrooms—It is imperative that the storage area be insect and rodent free, and that it be cool and dry.

Canning

Trim stems and discolored parts of mushrooms. Soak mushrooms in cold water for 10 minutes to remove adhering soil; drain, wash in clean water and drain again. Leave small mushrooms whole; cut larger ones in halves or quarters. Steam 4 minutes or heat gently for 15 minutes without added liquid in a covered saucepan.

For glass jars, pack hot mushrooms to 1/2 inch from the top. Add 1/4 teaspoon of salt to half pints; 1/2 teaspoon to pints. For better color, add crystalline ascorbic acid; 1/16 teaspoon to half pints and 1/8 teaspoon to pints. Add boiling hot cooking liquid or boiling water to cover mushrooms, leaving 1/2-inch space at top of jar. Process in pressure canner at 10 pounds pressure (240° F) for 30 minutes. Remove jars from canner and complete seals if closures are not self-sealing.

For tin cans, pack hot mushrooms to 1/4 inch from top of can. Add 1/4 teaspoon of salt to No. 1 cans; 1/2 teaspoon of salt to No. 2 cans. For better color add crystalline ascorbic acid; 1/16 teaspoon to No. 1 cans and 1/8 teaspoon to No. 2 cans. Fill to top with boiling water. Exhaust to 170° F (about 10 minutes) and seal cans. Process in pressure canner at 10 pounds pressure (240° F) for 30 minutes. (From *Home and Garden Bulletin No. 8* U.S. Department of Agriculture.)

Orange delight and meadow mushrooms are best for canning. Drop cleaned mushrooms in boiling water containing 1 tablespoon of vinegar and 1 teaspoon of salt per quart of water. Simmer 3 to 5 minutes. Fill jars to 1/2 inch from the top with mushrooms and cover with fresh boiling water. Add 1/2 tablespoon of lemon juice to preserve color. Seal according to type of lid used. Process in pressure cooker for 25 minutes at 10 pounds pressure. Mushrooms cannot be cold-packed as can some fruits.

COOKING WITH MUSHROOMS

Store mushrooms in the refrigerator. Do not clean if they are to be used within a day. For storing more than 1 day, clean and cook before storing. To clean, cut off soiled roots, peel if caps are tough and rub off fuzz or scales with a damp cloth. Leave small caps whole. Wash only if necessary, using a quick dip method. Drain and dry on paper towels. Slice stems, if they are tender, and cook with caps.

Shaggy manes and inky caps cannot be stored, even for a day. They mature too quickly and dissolve into ink within a few hours.

Mushrooms can be added to a variety of meats, poultry and fish dishes, and can be added to any of the mild-flavored vegetables, such as peas, spinach, zucchini and green beans. Here are a few tips for using them:

Most edible mushrooms are interchangeable in recipes.

Mushroom recipes frequently include butter, but a good quality margarine may be substituted.

Tender mushrooms will become tough with prolonged cooking.

Mushrooms can be enhanced with a bit of nutmeg. Care should be taken that not too much nutmeg is used—sprinkle just a few grains on the mushrooms.

Large frozen mushrooms often need to be cut up before using. They can be cut more easily while only partially thawed.

Dried mushrooms, either pieces or puree, can be granulated or powdered by crushing with a rolling pin. The powder can be used instead of flour for dredging meat before browning, or can be added to any of a variety of dishes.

The emerging button of the deadly amanita somewhat resembles a puffball. For this reason, be sure to cut all puffballs through the middle to determine whether or not there is an embryo mushroom forming inside. If there is one, throw the mushroom away. The puffball is unbroken white inside, with an appearance similar to a cut marshmallow.

HORS D'OEUVRES, SPREADS AND RELISHES

Rolled Puffball Sandwiches

2 tablespoons butter
1/2 pound puffballs, finely chopped
1 teaspoon flour
1/2 cup heavy cream
Salt and pepper
Nutmeg
Whole-wheat bread, sliced thin
Parsley

Melt butter in saucepan and add finely chopped mushrooms; cook for 5 minutes. Sprinkle flour on mushrooms, stir, add heavy cream and cook until thickened. Season to taste with salt, pepper and small dash of nutmeg. Cut crusts from thin slices of bread, spread with mushroom filling and roll up, fasten with toothpicks and chill for several hours. Before serving, remove toothpicks and tuck a sprig of parsley into each sandwich. This filling also makes a good dip.

Sandwich Spread

1/2 cup mushrooms, finely chopped
1 cup liver sausage, mashed
1 tablespoon margarine
1/2 teaspoon Worcestershire sauce
Seasoned (or regular) salt
Seasoned (or regular) pepper
Mayonnaise

Saute chopped mushrooms in margarine; combine with other ingredients and add just enough mayonnaise to bind the whole into spreading consistency.

Marinated Shaggy Manes

1/2 pound mushrooms, chopped
4 tablespoons olive oil
2 tablespoons white wine
1/2 teaspoon salt
1/8 teaspoon pepper
2 or 3 green onions, minced

Combine all ingredients and mix well. Allow to stand for 2 or 3 hours before using. To serve, spread on thinly sliced pieces of French bread cut in fancy shapes or on toast rounds.

Marinated Mushrooms

2 cups mushrooms, bite-sized
1 cup cooking oil
1/4 cup lemon juice
2 tablespoons chives, chopped
1/2 teaspoon salt
Nutmeg, few grains

Choose bite-sized fresh mushrooms and clean well. Combine all other ingredients and pour over mushrooms. Marinate at least 6 hours, turning mushrooms once each hour. Drain and serve on toothpicks.

Continental Mushroom Caviar

1 small onion,
  sliced and minced
2 tablespoons olive oil
1/2 pound mushrooms,
  chopped fine
Salt and pepper
1 tablespoon lemon juice
Wild chives, chopped
1 tablespoon sour cream
Nutmeg, trace

Fry the onion in the oil until soft and limp. Add mushrooms and cook until barely soft. Add remaining ingredients. Chill well before serving. This is nice served with thin tomato slices.

Cocktail Mushrooms

Mushroom caps
Cream cheese
Ham
Mayonnaise
Seasonings

Fill perfect mushroom caps with seasoned cream cheese or ham or a mixture of both, moistened with mayonnaise. The mushrooms may be either raw or sauteed.

SOUPS AND STOCKS

Mushroom Base
Clean (but do not wash unless necessary) firm, fresh mushrooms of any edible species. Cut off bruised or tough lower portions of stems. Chop fine and saute in butter until all moisture is absorbed. Season lightly with

nutmeg and onion salt. Add a little Madeira wine. Cover and store in the refrigerator as a base for sauces or soups or to add to sauces, gravies, stews and vegetables. Also useful as the moistening agent in meat loaf or stuffing.

Mushroom Stock

Mushrooms, any edible species
Water
Wild chives (or onions)
Salt and pepper

Clean the mushrooms, cut into small pieces and place in large kettle. Add an equal amount of water and a handful of minced wild chives. Salt and pepper to taste. Simmer gently for about 2 hours. Strain while still hot. The stock makes an excellent base for gravies, soups and sauces. The pieces of mushrooms that were strained out of the stock are good in meat loaf, stew, gravy and soup. They can be left in the stock if you prefer.

Frozen Mushroom Stock

Clean mushroom bits and pieces, including stems, and cook them slowly for about 2 hours. A few celery leaves or a bit of chopped parsley adds to the flavor. Strain, cool and pour into rigid plastic containers; freeze for future use in soups, gravies and stews.

Mushroom Bouillon

1/2 pound any edible mushrooms
4 cups water or consomme
1 tablespoon tops of chives, finely chopped
1/2 teaspoon grated green onion
Salt
Sherry

Simmer mushrooms and the liquid for an hour. Add the grated onion and salt and cook 10 minutes more. Let stand overnight. Strain and serve hot or cold. Add a spoonful of finely chopped raw mushrooms and a few drops of sherry to each bouillon cup before filling.

Jellied Mushroom Soup

3 cups consomme or stock
2 cups mushrooms, coarsely chopped
1 envelope unflavored gelatin
1/2 cup water
1/4 lemon, peeled
1 piece lemon peel, about 2 inches
1/4 cup white wine
Salt and pepper
1/2 cup yogurt
Chives, minced

Simmer the consomme and mushrooms gently for 15 to 20 minutes. Soak gelatin in water until dissolved. Add lemon peel and lemon pulp to the gelatin and liquefy in a blender for 20 seconds. Add mushrooms and consomme; puree for 20 seconds. Add wine and seasonings; stir for 10 seconds. Chill until serving time. Serve with a dollop of yogurt and garnish with minced green chives.

Chinese Chicken Soup

1/2 cup egg noodles
2 tablespoons granulated chicken bouillon (or cubes)
1/2 cup green onion tops, chopped
1 tablespoon minced dry onions
1/2 cup diced celery
1 cup mushrooms, coarsely chopped
Salt and pepper to taste
1 teaspoon parsley flakes
4 cups hot water

Cook noodles with bouillon (bouillon granules dissolved in the hot water) until brought to a boil. Add onion tops, parsley flakes and celery. Reduce heat and simmer slowly for 15 minutes, then add mushrooms and cook gently for another 10 minutes. Season to taste. Sprinkle a few of the parsley flakes on top of each serving. A sprinkling of paprika can be used also if you wish.

Cream of Mushroom Soup I

Thin white sauce
Mushrooms
Margarine
Onion salt
Seasoned pepper

Saute the mushrooms in the margarine briefly. Put through a blender or sieve to make a puree. Season the thin white sauce with onion salt and pepper; add the puree. Serve with croutons. Make this soup as thin or as thick as your personal preference dictates. Puffballs are probably the easiest to handle for this dish. Before sauteeing, cut them into fairly small pieces so that all mushrooms will be done at the same time.

Cream of Mushroom Soup II

Mushrooms
Thin cream
Chicken bouillon cubes (optional)
Salt and pepper

Put mushrooms and cream through the blender and add more cream. Heat and season to taste. Add bouillon cubes if desired and stir to dissolve.

Cream of Mushroom Soup III

Mushrooms	Flour
Stock or bouillon	Milk
Butter	Cheese, bacon, chives or parsley

Simmer chopped mushrooms in chicken or beef stock (or bouillon). In another pan, mix equal quantities of butter and flour over medium heat. Stirring constantly, add milk until thickened to soup consistency. Add mushrooms and stock; thicken more if necessary. Garnish with grated cheese, crumbled bacon, chopped chives or parsley.

SALADS AND DRESSINGS

Mushrooms are good raw in salads—just clean and slice. A few drops of lemon juice should keep them from turning color after being cut. Leftover liquor from marinating mushrooms makes an excellent base for various salad dressings. Experiment a bit.

Tossed Salad With Mushrooms

Lettuce	Tomato
Celery	Salt and pepper
Green onions	Mushrooms, uncooked (puffballs)
Cucumber	Oil and vinegar dressing

Tear lettuce into pieces, mince green onions, slice tomato and cut celery into bite-sized pieces. Slice or coarsely chop the mushrooms. Season to your taste and serve with oil and vinegar dressing. A nice addition to this is peeled and sliced wild cow parsnip and/or fresh fireweed shoots, if readily available.

Combination Salad

1 cup sliced mushrooms, sauteed	1/4 cup carrots, sliced and cooked
1/2 cup green beans, cooked	Favorite salad dressing
1/2 cup whole kernel corn, cooked	Seasoning to taste
1/2 cup asparagus or broccoli, cooked	Lettuce
Chives, fresh and minced	

Combine all ingredients and serve on crisp lettuce.

Mushroom Spinach Salad

Spinach, fresh and crisp
Mushrooms
Salt and pepper
Oil and vinegar dressing

Tear spinach into bite-sized pieces. Clean mushrooms and slice those that are a bit too large; leave smaller ones whole. Season with a dash of salt and pepper. Serve with oil and vinegar dressing.

Puffball Salad

French dressing
Puffballs
Salt and pepper
Herbs to taste
Lettuce

Have French dressing ready in a bowl. Clean and slice firm fresh puffballs into the dressing. This will keep them from discoloring. Season to taste. Herbs that are good with this salad include wild chives, thyme and basil. You may wish to experiment with others. Let salad stand in the refrigerator for at least 2 hours. Drain any excess liquid and serve salad in a nest of lettuce leaves. Salty crackers are good with this.

SAUCES AND GRAVIES

Mushroom Sauce

1 cup mushrooms
3 tablespoons butter
3 tablespoons flour
1-1/2 cups milk or stock
1/2 teaspoon salt
1/8 teaspoon nutmeg
Pepper to taste
2 egg yolks, beaten
2 teaspoons lemon juice

Brown the mushrooms in the butter and add the flour; blend well. Add the milk, salt, nutmeg and pepper. Cook slowly until thick. Gently stir in the egg yolks and lemon juice. Cook 2 minutes longer. Serve at once.

Mushroom Garlic Sauce

1/4 cup olive oil
2 cloves garlic, split
1 cup sauteed mushrooms

Heat the olive oil with the garlic cloves. Remove the garlic and add the mushrooms. Reheat if necessary. This is good served with spaghetti.

Paprika Sauce

2 onions, chopped
4 tablespoons butter
1 tablespoon whole-wheat flour
1/2 cup puffballs, chopped coarsely

Salt to taste
1 tablespoon paprika
1 cup sour cream

Cook the onions in the butter until golden. Remove from skillet and cook the mushrooms for 3 minutes Return onions to skillet and stir in flour and seasoning. Add the cream and cook and stir until smooth and thick.

Mushroom and Tomato Sauce

2 tablespoons butter
2 tablespoons flour
1 cup tomato juice
Salt and pepper

Onion powder
Oregano
1 cup sliced mushrooms, sauteed

Melt butter and stir in flour; slowly add the tomato juice. Add seasonings to taste. Cook and stir over low heat until thickened. Add the mushrooms.

Spaghetti Sauce With Mushrooms

4 onions, thinly sliced
6 tablespoons margarine
2 pounds mushrooms, sliced
Salt and pepper

1/4 teaspoon nutmeg
1 cup heavy cream
Spaghetti

Melt half the margarine in a heavy skillet and saute onions until they are golden brown, about 5 to 7 minutes over medium heat. Stir frequently to keep from overcooking. Reduce heat to low; cover skillet and cook slowly for 30 minutes; stir occasionally. The onions should be soft and mushy. Melt remaining margarine in another skillet and saute the mushrooms until tender. Season and add to the onions. Keep the sauce hot while you cook the spaghetti. Five minutes before serving time, add cream to sauce and heat but **DO NOT BOIL** or sauce will curdle. Blend spaghetti and sauce and serve. Sprinkle with grated Parmesan cheese if desired.

Mushroom Gravy

Saute any species of edible mushroom in butter. Add liquid and mushrooms to chicken broth or any meat drippings and thicken with flour, cornstarch or arrowroot as you would any gravy. Season to taste.

Mushroom Meat Sauce

2 cups mushrooms
4 tablespoons butter
3 tablespoons flour

1/2 to 1 cup meat drippings
Water

Saute mushrooms in butter briefly. Sprinkle flour over the mushrooms. Add enough water to the meat drippings to make 2 cups. Add this to the mushroom mixture. Stir and cook slowly until thick and smooth. Pour mushroom sauce over ham, chops, turkey, fish, steaks or roast meat for serving.

LIGHT MEALS

Scrambled Morels and Eggs

1 cup morel mushrooms
2 eggs
2 tablespoons milk
Margarine

Salt and pepper

Chop the mushrooms coarsely and saute briefly in margarine. Beat the eggs until light; season to taste. Add the milk and beat again. Pour the egg mixture over the morels and stir gently just until the egg mixture is cooked. Serve with hot toast and wild strawberry jam.

Sulphur polypore mushrooms may be substituted for morels for somewhat cheese-flavored scrambled eggs.

Eggs With Mushrooms

2 tablespoons olive oil
1 tablespoon green onion, minced
1 tablespoon parsley, chopped fine
1 pound mushrooms, sliced thin
1 tablespoon flour

1/2 cup dry white wine
Salt and pepper
6 eggs, hard-boiled and chopped coarsely

Cook onion and parsley in hot olive oil for 2 minutes. Add mushrooms and cover; simmer gently over low heat for about 10 minutes. Stir in flour and wine. Cover and simmer for 5 minutes more. Season to taste. Add eggs, cover and simmer for 5 minutes longer, stirring occasionally. Serve with hot garlic French bread.

OMELETS AND SOUFFLES

Mushroom Omelet I

4 eggs
1/4 cup water
1/2 teaspoon salt
Chives, minced

1/8 teaspoon pepper
2 tablespoons butter
Creamed or sauteed mushrooms

Beat eggs just enough to mingle whites and yolks. Add water and salt, pepper and chives. Melt the butter in an omelet pan or frying pan with sloping sides. Swirl the butter around in the pan to make sure all sides and the bottom are coated. Reduce heat and add the beaten eggs at once. Lift the edges of the omelet as it cooks so that uncooked portion can run underneath. Cook until creamy. Increase heat just enough to brown the omelet underneath slightly. Remove to a hot platter and pour either creamed or sauteed mushrooms over eggs. Fold into half-moon shape. Serve with wild currant jelly.

Mushroom Omelet II

4 large eggs
4 tablespoons milk
Salt and pepper
1/2 cup finely chopped mushrooms, broiled or sauteed

1 tablespoon butter
Herbs to taste

Beat the eggs just enough to mix the yolks and whites well. Add the milk, salt and pepper and the finely chopped mushrooms. Stir enough to mix. Melt the butter in the omelet pan and swirl around to coat the sides as well as bottom of pan. Pour omelet mixture into pan and cook slowly, lifting cooked edges with spatula to allow uncooked portion to run underneath. Cook only until eggs are set. Fold into a half-moon shape and serve on a hot platter surrounded by sprigs of parsley and dabs of wild berry jelly.

Mushroom Souffle

2 tablespoons butter
3 tablespoons flour
1/2 cup milk
1/2 cup mushroom liquor
1/2 teaspoon salt
3 egg whites, beaten stiff

3 egg yolks, beaten
1 cup mushrooms, coarsely chopped

Cook mushroom pieces in a little water until almost tender. Drain and set aside. Make a white sauce of the butter, flour, liquids and salt. Blend slowly into the egg yolks and add the mushroom pieces. Fold in the egg whites carefully. Pour into ungreased casserole. Set the casserole in a pan of hot water and bake in a 350° oven until a knife inserted into the souffle comes out clean. Tiny Petersburg shrimp may be added to the souffle just before folding in the egg whites.

FRIED MUSHROOMS

Basic Recipe

Saute sliced onions in bacon fat; add chopped mushrooms and cook over medium heat for 15 to 20 minutes.

Breaded Mushrooms

Mushrooms, sliced
1 egg, beaten
Butter or olive oil

Bread or cracker crumbs
Cheese, finely grated
Salt to taste

Combine crumbs, cheese and salt. Dip mushroom slices in beaten egg, then in crumb mixture. Fry in hot butter or olive oil until brown.

Sauteed Mushrooms

1 pound mushrooms
  (puffballs or boletes)
1/4 cup butter

Salt and pepper
Nutmeg, merest trace

Clean and slice puffballs or boletes. Melt the butter in a large, heavy skillet and heat to medium hot. Put in the mushrooms and seasonings. Reduce heat, cover and cook over low heat for 10 minutes.

Mushroom Fritters

Stock
Mushroom caps
Fritter batter

Mayonnaise
Chopped herbs

Bring the stock to a boil and blanch the mushrooms in it. Then dip them in a thick fritter batter. Fry and serve with herbed mayonnaise (simply chop your choice of fresh herbs finely and add to the mayonnaise).

Saucepan Mushrooms

Mushrooms, sliced
Butter and olive oil,
  equal amounts
  (vegetable oil may be substituted)

Optional:
Dry white wine
Parsley, chopped
Garlic, chopped

Cook mushrooms in butter/oil combination in saucepan for a few minutes on high heat. Reduce heat and, if desired, add a little dry white wine a few minutes before mushrooms are done. Serve plain, or add chopped parsley and garlic.

CREAMED MUSHROOMS

Basic Recipe

Mushrooms; whole if small,
  sliced or chopped if large
1 tablespoon flour

1 cup light cream
Nutmeg
Sherry

Saute mushrooms, sprinkle with flour and add cream. Cook until slightly thickened and season to taste with nutmeg and sherry.

Variation

1 cup mushrooms
Butter
White sauce

Chives, chopped
Parsley, chopped
Cheese, grated

Prepare your favorite white sauce recipe. Saute mushrooms in butter and add to white sauce. Serve alone sprinkled with chives or parsley and grated cheese. May be served over cauliflower, peas, fish or other seafood, ham or tongue.

Creamed Mushrooms in Potato Nests

3 cups hot mashed potatoes,
  seasoned
2 tablespoons cream
1 tablespoon butter, melted
1 tablespoon onion juice
  or 1 teaspoon onion powder
1 egg, slightly beaten
1 teaspoon baking powder

3 cups mushrooms, diced
3 tablespoons butter
1/2 teaspoon salt
1/4 teaspoon pepper
3 tablespoons flour
1 cup milk
1/2 cup cream
2 tablespoons sherry

Combine potatoes, 2 tablespoons cream, onion juice and egg. Beat until light, then add baking powder and again beat well. On well-greased cookie sheet, shape potato mixture into nests, hollowing out centers with a tablespoon and swirling edges with a fork. Brush with melted butter and bake at 400° to 450° until golden brown, 15 to 20 minutes. Lift nests to hot platter with a spatula and fill with hot creamed mixture. Cook the mushrooms in 3 tablespoons butter until just tender; add seasoning and flour and blend smoothly. Add the milk and 1/2 cup cream. Bring to boiling point, stirring constantly; cook for 5 minutes. Add the sherry just before pouring into nests.

Creamed Mushrooms and Ham

2 cups mushrooms
Salted water
Lemon juice, dash
1 cup cooked ham, cubed

Medium white sauce
Chives, wild, or onions, minced
Pepper
Chow mein noodles or toast

Cook cleaned and sliced puffballs, or other edible mushrooms, in the salted water to which the dash of lemon juice has been added. When tender (it won't take long), remove from heat and drain liquid. If some of the slices are rather large, you might chop them a bit at this point. Chop cooked ham into half-inch cubes. Combine both ham and mushrooms with the medium white sauce. Add a few bits of minced wild chives and a little pepper. Serve over chow mein noodles, toast or hot biscuits.

BROILED AND BAKED DISHES

Broiled Mushrooms

Brush medium-sized caps with melted butter and place in shallow pan about 3 inches from the heat source. Season with salt, pepper and nutmeg. Broil 8 to 10 minutes. Serve with a variety of dishes.

Baked Mushrooms

1 cup milk
1 cup grated cheese
1 tablespoon grated onion
1 teaspoon salt

1/4 teaspoon dry mustard
Spinach, cooked
1-1/2 pounds mushrooms

Combine the milk, cheese, onion, salt and dry mustard. Line a buttered casserole with the cooked spinach. Fill with the mushrooms and pour the milk mixture over all. Bake in a 350° oven for 30 minutes or until mushrooms are tender.

Baked Shaggy Mane

Cut cleaned mushrooms lengthwise. Place on baking pan, cut side up. Season with salt, pepper and butter. Bake at 325° for 3 to 5 minutes.

Mushroom-Sour Cream Casserole

4 cups chopped mushrooms	1 cup chopped parsley
2 cups bread crumbs	1 small onion, minced
(or crumbled saltine crackers)	1 cup sour cream
2/3 cup butter	Salt and pepper to taste

Butter casserole baking dish, sprinkle bread crumbs on bottom, place a layer of mushrooms on top and dot with butter. Add another layer of crumbs, sprinkle with parsley and onion and dot with butter. Repeat layers, ending with crumbs dotted with butter. Bake 20 minutes at 350°; cover with sour cream and continue baking for 10 minutes.

Chicken-Mushroom Casserole

1 can chow mein noodles	3/4 cup onion, chopped
(or crumbled saltine crackers	2 cups mushrooms, chopped
or bread crumbs)	2 cups mushroom soup
2 cups cooked chicken	1 cup cashews or almonds
1 cup celery, chopped	Cheese, grated

Spread chow mein noodles (cracker or bread crumbs) over bottom of baking dish. In a bowl, combine cooked chicken, celery, onion, mushrooms, mushroom soup and nuts. Pour mixture over noodles and sprinkle grated cheese over the top. Bake at 350° (325° for glass pan) for 15 to 20 minutes, or until heated through.

Scalloped Mushrooms With Ham

3 tablespoons margarine	4 tablespoons butter, melted
4 tablespoons flour	6 eggs, hard-boiled and sliced
1/2 teaspoon salt	1 cup ham, cubed
2 cups milk	3/4 cup mushrooms, sliced
1 cup dry bread crumbs	

Make white sauce of margarine, flour, salt and milk. Moisten crumbs with melted butter. In a greased casserole alternate layers of crumbs, eggs, ham and mushrooms. Pour the white sauce over the top layer and top with more crumbs. Bake at 350° for 20 to 25 minutes.

Mushroom Fondue Bake

Mushrooms, cut into thick slices
Butter and olive oil, equal amounts
  (vegetable oil may be substituted)
Cheese, sliced
Sour cream
Salt

Grease a baking pan with butter. Spread mushroom slices in pan, salt lightly, then cover with cheese slices. Alternate several layers of mushrooms and cheese. Bake in 275° oven. When mushrooms are half done and cheese is melted, pour sour cream over all and continue baking until surface is golden brown.

Mushroom Bake

Mushroom caps
Salt
Pepper
Butter
Cream
Toast

Reserve the mushroom stems for use in making Mushroom Base stock (page 249). Put the caps in a shallow baking pan, smooth side down. Sprinkle with salt and pepper and dot with butter. Pour a little cream around them. Bake for 10 minutes in a 450° oven. You may need to add a little more cream before the mushrooms are done baking. Place on buttered toast and pour the pan juices over them.

Green Bean Casserole

1 quart green snap beans
1 quart water
1 cup coarsely chopped
  mushrooms
6 tablespoons margarine
Onions, dried minced
1 cup half-inch ham cubes
Salt
Red pepper, crushed

Bring beans to a boil in large kettle; reduce heat to simmer. Add ham, seasonings and onions. Simmer slowly for 2 hours or more. Check occasionally to be sure there is enough water on the beans, add more if needed. The beans should be soft and most of the water cooked away when they are done. While the beans are cooking, saute the mushrooms in the margarine. When the beans are thoroughly cooked, drain off all but 1/2 cup of water. Put cooked beans in casserole and cover with the sauteed mushrooms. A little grated cheese may be sprinkled on top if desired. Bake in a 300° oven for 30 minutes.

A little mushroom soup mixed with the beans adds to the flavor and may be used.

Mushroom Mold

3 tablespoons butter
2 tablespoons onion, finely chopped
3/4 pound mushrooms, coarsely chopped
Salt and pepper to taste
2 to 3 tablespoons whole-wheat flour
1/2 cup milk
2 eggs, beaten well
Nutmeg

Melt butter in heavy skillet and add the chopped onion. Cook slowly until golden brown. Add the mushrooms and cook and stir for 5 minutes. Add seasonings to taste (go lightly on the nutmeg). Sprinkle with the flour and gradually add the milk while stirring. Cook until thick and add the beaten eggs. Stir just to blend well. Pour into buttered ring mold and bake at 350° until firm (30 to 40 minutes). Turn onto platter and fill the center with buttered green peas.

Fiddlehead Ferns With Mushrooms and Chicken

2 cups boiling water
1 teaspoon salt
2 cups Alaska fiddlehead ferns, fresh or frozen
3 tablespoons margarine
3 tablespoons flour
1 cup mushroom pieces, sauteed
1 cup chicken broth or stock
2-1/2 to 3 cups chicken, cooked and sliced
2 tablespoons parsley
2 tablespoons bread crumbs

Cook fiddleheads in boiling water for 1 minute; reduce heat and simmer until tender. Mix margarine and flour in saucepan and cook briefly over medium heat, blending well. Stir in the broth and keep stirring until sauce is thick and smooth. Stir in any juice left over from cooking mushrooms. Add mushroom pieces and season to taste. Arrange drained fiddleheads in a large casserole and cover with the chicken slices. Pour the sauce over the chicken. Sprinkle crumbs on top and also add a sprinkling of parsley. Bake uncovered for 15 to 25 minutes in a 375° oven. When done it should be brown and bubbly.

Brussels sprouts, asparagus or broccoli may be substituted for the fiddlehead.

Potatoes Au Gratin With Mushrooms

Potatoes
Mushrooms, finely chopped
Bread crumbs
Butter
Salt and pepper
Cheese, grated

Boil unpeeled potatoes in salted water; drain, peel and slice. Arrange layer of potatoes in baking dish, add layer of mushrooms, sprinkle with salt and pepper, cover with bread crumbs and dot with butter. Repeat layers, ending with crumbs and butter, then sprinkle grated cheese over the top. Bake in 325° to 350° oven until surface is lightly browned.

Mushroom-Potato Pie

Potatoes
Seasoning
Cheese, grated
Mushrooms, sauteed
Chives, minced
Paprika

Cook and mash potatoes and season to taste. Saute the mushrooms in a little margarine and add them to the mashed potatoes. Stir. Put the mixture in a well-greased casserole and sprinkle with minced chives, grated cheese and paprika. Bake in a 350° oven until the top is well browned.

You might also try half sweet potatoes and half white potatoes sometime in this recipe.

Casserole Supreme

1/4 cup butter
1 cup onion, finely chopped
2 cups shaggy mane mushrooms
1 cup milk
1 cup homemade mushroom soup
2 pounds broccoli, fresh or frozen
Salt and pepper
2 cups ham, cubed
1-1/2 cups commercial stuffing mix

Saute onions in butter until limp; add mushrooms and saute briefly until mushrooms are tender. Stir in milk and soup. Put one-third of the broccoli in a deep, well-greased casserole. Sprinkle with seasonings and put one-third of ham, sauce and stuffing mix on top. Repeat until all ingredients are used. Bake in a 350° oven for 30 minutes or until broccoli is tender.

Brussels sprouts or asparagus may be used instead of broccoli.

STUFFED MUSHROOMS

With Nuts

1-1/2 pounds large mushrooms
Onion flakes, dry and minced
1/4 cup margarine
1 cup soft bread crumbs
1 cup Brazil nuts
  or filberts, ground

Salt and pepper
1 tablespoon ketchup
1 tablespoon lemon juice
3 strips bacon
1/2 cup cream

Clean mushrooms and remove stems. Cook chopped stems and onion in margarine for 5 minutes. Add crumbs and nuts; cook 2 minutes more. Add seasonings. Stuff mushrooms with the mixture and place in baking dish. Cut bacon in smaller strips and garnish stuffed mushrooms with them. Pour the cream so that it surrounds the mushrooms. Bake in 400° oven for 20 to 25 minutes.

With Spinach

1 pound mushrooms,
  approximately
2 tablespoons cooking oil
2 cups spinach, packed
2 garlic cloves, minced

2 egg whites, beaten slightly
1/2 teaspoon salt
1/4 teaspoon pepper
1/2 cup commercial bread crumbs
  with Italian seasonings

Clean mushrooms and separate caps from stems. Saute the caps in oil. Chop the stems except for the tough ends. Cook spinach and chopped stems in a small amount of water until spinach is done. Drain thoroughly and combine with egg whites and bread crumbs. Stuff mushroom caps with the mixture. Put caps in shallow, well-oiled baking dish and bake at 350° in a preheated oven for about 15 minutes.

With Chives

8 to 10 large mushrooms,
  cap varieties
1-1/2 tablespoons minced chives
2 tablespoons lemon juice

1 tablespoon mayonnaise
1 tablespoon olive oil
1-1/2 teaspoons lemon pepper
1 teaspoon salt

Clean and wipe large, firm mushrooms. Remove stems and discard the tough lower ends. Chop the upper parts of stems finely. Combine all ingredients except the mushroom caps. Stuff the caps with the mixture and bake in a shallow, oiled pan for 10 minutes in a 450° oven.

With Sausage

Clean mushrooms and peel if necessary. Caps should be large for stuffing. Stuff with seasoned country sausage and arrange on broiler pan. Broil under low heat for about 20 minutes. Serve on rounds of buttered toast.

MUSHROOM SPECIALTIES

Mushrooms a la France

Mushrooms	Salt and pepper
Bread crusts	Butter
Stock	1 egg, slightly beaten
Dry white wine	Yolk of hard-boiled egg

Saute mushrooms in a bit of butter. In another pan, soak some bread crusts in a mixture of half stock and half white wine. Season with salt and pepper to taste. Cook slowly, then strain off any liquor and add a little butter and a slightly beaten egg to make a good thick white sauce. Taste and correct seasoning. Add the sauce to the mushrooms. Put hard-boiled egg yolk through sieve and sprinkle sieved yolk on each serving.

Chicken Livers and Mushrooms

1 slice lean bacon, diced	1 cup chicken bouillon
2 tablespoons butter	1 teaspoon lemon juice
1 green onion, diced	1/2 cup sliced puffballs
1 pound chicken or rabbit livers	Parsley, finely chopped
2 tablespoons whole-wheat flour	

Cook bacon and butter together for 5 minutes. Add the diced green onion, tops and all, and cook 2 minutes more. Add the chicken livers and cook another 2 minutes. Sprinkle the flour over the mixture and add the bouillon, lemon juice and mushrooms. Cook another 2 minutes or until slightly thickened. Sprinkle with finely chopped parsley before serving.

Mushroom Goulash

1 large onion, diced	1/2 cup canned whole kernel corn
2 tablespoons butter	1 bay leaf
1 quart mushrooms	1 tablespoon parsley, chopped
1-1/2 cups canned tomatoes	Salt and pepper
1/2 cup sour cream	

Brown the onion in the butter and add the mushrooms; simmer for 5 minutes. Add the remainder of the ingredients except for sour cream and stir to mingle. Reheat just before serving and add the sour cream.

We like to crumble and brown in fat a little ground moose and stir this into the goulash. It is a great way to make a little burger go a long way.

Mushrooms and Barley

1/2 pound slice puffballs
8 tablespoons margarine
1 cup wild chives, chopped
1-1/2 cups pearl barley

3 cups chicken or
   mushroom stock
Pepper

Cook the puffballs (or other edible mushrooms) in 4 tablespoons melted margarine in a moderately hot skillet for about 5 minutes. Set aside. Cook the chopped tops of the wild chives in the remainder of the butter until they are wilted but not browned. Add the barley and stir over medium heat just until the barley is browned. (Watch it carefully; do not allow it to become too brown.) Put in a greased casserole with the mushrooms and 1-1/2 cups chicken or mushroom stock. (Chicken stock may be made from commercial bouillon.) Cover the casserole and bake in a 350° oven for 30 minutes. Add another 1-1/2 cups of the stock and sprinkle lightly with pepper. Bake 30 minutes longer. If it seems too dry you may need to add still more stock. The casserole is done when the barley is tender but not mushy. Avoid overcooking.

Mushroom Stew Supreme

1 pound mushrooms
1/4 cup olive oil
1 tablespoon chives, chopped fine
1 teaspoon fennel seed

2 tablespoons parsley, chopped
Juice of 1 small lemon
Salt and pepper
1/2 cup dry white wine

Clean and trim mushrooms as needed. Saute in warm olive oil with chives, fennels seeds and parsley for 5 to 8 minutes. Sprinkle lemon juice over mushrooms and season as desired. Cook for 3 minutes longer. Add wine, cover and simmer gently for 5 minutes more. Excellent with game.

Stuffed Tomatoes

Onions, chopped
Mushrooms, chopped
Spinach, cooked,
   drained and chopped

Garlic salt
Parmesan cheese, grated
Olive oil
Tomatoes

Saute chopped onions and mushrooms until just soft. Mix with the drained cooked spinach and garlic salt. Add grated Parmesan cheese to taste. Cut a slice off the stem end of tomatoes and scoop out most of the pulp. Discard all seeds. Sprinkle insides of tomatoes with salt. Turn upside down and allow to stand for 30 minutes. Then stuff the tomatoes with the mixture and put in a buttered pan. Sprinkle with bread crumbs if desired. Bake at 400° for 20 minutes.

Mushrooms Italian Style

1 pound mushrooms, sliced thin
3 tablespoons olive oil
1/2 clove garlic
Salt and pepper
1 tablespoon butter

4 or 5 anchovy fillets
 chopped small
2 tablespoons parsley,
 chopped fine
Juice of 1/2 lemon

Brown garlic in the olive oil heated in a large skillet. Remove the garlic. Place mushrooms, salt and pepper in the skillet and saute over high heat until any mushroom liquor has evaporated. Add the butter, anchovies and parsley and cook over reduced heat 5 minutes more. Remove from heat and add lemon juice. Serve hot.

Mushroom and Wild Rice Stuffing

1 cup wild rice
2 tablespoons cooking oil
1/2 pound mushrooms, chopped

1/4 cup chopped onion
Salt and pepper
Nutmeg, trace

Steam rice until tender. Cook the mushrooms and onion together in the butter for 5 minutes. Add mixture to the rice. Season to taste with salt, pepper and nutmeg. Stuff fowl loosely and bake as usual.

Mushroom Balls With Meat

Mushrooms, cubed
Butter
Olive oil
Salt and pepper
Flour

Meat, cooked and chopped
Broth or bouillon
Egg, beaten
Bread or cracker crumbs

Cook mushroom cubes in equal amounts of butter and olive oil; season with salt and pepper to taste. Combine mushrooms with meat, broth and sufficient flour to bind together; form mixture into balls and roll in egg and crumbs. Fry in very hot oil, drain and serve.

Chapter 9
Field Notes

The information in this chapter will be useful to collectors in hunting mushrooms in the field. It includes a statistical summary of the mushrooms—How many of each kind? How many white?—so that the newcomer to mushroom hunting will know what to expect. There is also a suggested form for keeping field notes, and check lists of the mushrooms so the collector can keep track of what he or she has seen.

STATISTICAL SUMMARY

This book lists the 101 commonest of the 500 mushrooms found in Alaska. The 101 species are of 9 families, divided further into 52 genera, and distributed in the book as follows:

GILLED MUSHROOMS, FAMILY *AGARICACEAE:*
Chapter 5—Those with spores colorless, white,
  cream, yellow or buff.........................18 genera, 41 species
Chapter 6—Those with spores NOT colorless, white,
  cream, yellow or buff..........................13 genera, 25 species

MUSHROOMS WITHOUT GILLS:
Chapter 7—8 families ....21 genera, 35 species
  Fleshy pore fungi, family *Boletaceae*.......................7 species
  Woody pore fungi, family *Polyporaceae* ....4 species
  Toothed, or hedgehog, fungi, family *Hydnaceae* ....4 species
  Club, or coral, fungi, family *Clavariaceae* ....7 species
  Sac, or sponge, fungi, family *Helvellaceae* ....6 species
  Puffballs, or stomach fungi, family *Lycoperdaceae* ....3 species
  Cup fungi, family *Pezizaceae* ....3 species
  Earth tongues, family *Geoglossaceae* ....1 species

Two of the more important things to know about mushrooms are their edibility and the colors of their spores. Our interest in edibility needs little explanation: We want to know which mushrooms are good to eat. (Most of them are.) Spore color, however, is at least as important, because it is a chief means of identification of mushrooms. Edibility and spore color among the 101 mushrooms are summarized as follows:

	Number of species
EDIBILITY:	
Edible	68

Species 4, 5-8, 10, 11-14, 16, 23, 28-33, 36, 38, 41-45, 48, 49, 51, 53-60, 62-75, 78-80, 82-86, 88, 92, 93, 95-101

Questionable or edibility unknown 15
Species 22, 24-27, 37, 39, 46, 47, 52, 61, 76, 77, 81, 87

Inedible or dangerous........ 11
Species 3, 9, 15, 17, 18, 20, 34, 35, 40, 91, 94

Poisonous 7
Species 1, 2, 19, 21, 50, 89, 90

SPORE COLOR:
Colorless 2
Species 6 and 79

White, whitish 45
Species 1-4, 7-15, 17-31, 33-35, 37-41, 74, 75, 77, 78, 84, 86, 90, 91

Cream, creamy white, yellowish white............................. 2
Species 5, 16 and 76

Whitish yellow, pale yellow 3
Species 32, 36, 94

Yellow, yellowish.. 3
Species 89, 92, 93

Buff, yellow-buff, yellow-brown..................................... 8
Species 50-55, 82, 83

Yellow-brown (rusty) 5
Species 44-48

Olive-brown... 9
Species 67-72, 95-97

Ochraceous, pale ocher, yellowish orange 3
Species 49, 87, 88

Pink, salmon, brownish salmon....................2
Species 42 and 43

Purple-brown 6
Species 56-61

Brown, brownish...4
Species 62, 73, 80, 81

Black 4
Species 63-66

Spore color unknown 4
Species 98-101

A FORM FOR FIELD NOTES

It is useful to keep notes on the mushrooms you find, for at least two reasons. One, you'd like to return to the same site and gather mushrooms again; you don't want to forget where you found them. And two, notes on a past find may help you identify the mushroom you find today.

Here's a form for field notes that could easily be put in a pocket notebook.

COLLECTOR'S FIELD NOTES

Name of mushroom:_____ Date:_____

Habit:_____

Habitat:_____

Location:_____

Special notes, photographic data, etc.:_____

_____

CHECK LIST OF GILLED MUSHROOMS—FAMILY AGARICACEAE—WITH SPORES COLORLESS, WHITE, CREAM, YELLOW OR BUFF
Species 1 through 41

Genus *Amanita*
 1. *Amanita muscaria,* fly agaric; poisonous. Spores white.
 2. *Amanita porphyria,* purple-brown amanita; poisonous. Spores white.
 3. *Amanita (Amanitopsis) vaginata,* sheathed amanitopsis, grisette; edible, but dangerous. Spores white.

Genus *Armillariella (Armillaria)*
 4. *Armillariella (Armillaria) mellea,* honey mushroom; edible. Spores white.

Genus *Cantharellus*
 5. *Cantharellus tubaeformis,* tubelike chantarelle; edible with caution. Spores yellowish white.

Genus *Catathelasma*
 6. *Catathelasma imperialis;* edible, but may be unpalatable. Spores colorless.

Genus *Clitocybe (Lyophyllum)*
 7. *Clitocybe multiceps (Lyophyllum decastes),* fried chicken mushroom; edible. Spores white.

Genus *Collybia*
 8. *Collybia acervata;* edible. Spores white.
 9. *Collybia dryophila;* inedible to some people; dangerous. Spores white.

Genus *Flammulina (Collybia)*
 10. *Flammulina (Collybia) velutipes,* velvet-stemmed mushroom; edible. Spores white.

Genus *Hygrophorus*
 11. *Hygrophorus conicus,* cone-shaped waxy cap; edible to most people. Spores white.
 12. *Hygrophorus chrysodon;* edible. Spores white.
 13. *Hygrophorus eburneus;* edible. Spores white.

Genus *Laccaria*
 14. *Laccaria laccata;* edible. Spores white.

Genus *Lactarius*
15. *Lactarius controversus,* controversial milky cap; inedible. Spores white.
16. *Lactarius deliciosus,* orange delight, orange milky cap; edible. Spores pale cream.
17. *Lactarius mucidus,* slimy milky cap; inedible. Spores white.
18. *Lactarius representaneus;* inedible. Spores white.
19. *Lactarius rufus;* poisonous. Spores white.
20. *Lactarius scrobiculatus;* inedible. Spores white.
21. *Lactarius torminosus,* woolly milky cap; poisonous. Spores white.

Genus *Lepiota*
22. *Lepiota clypeolaria;* edibility unknown; may be poisonous. Spores white.

Genus *Leucopaxillus (Clitocybe)*
23. *Leucopaxillus (Clitocybe) giganteus*; edible. Spores white.

Genus *Limacella*
24. *Limacella illinita;* edibility unknown. Spores white.

Genus *Marasmius*
25. *Marasmius androsaceus;* edibility unknown. Spores white.
26. *Marasmius epiphyllus;* edibility unkown. Spores white.

Genus *Mycena*
27. *Mycena pura;* edibility questionable; edible for some persons, but not all. Spores white.

Genus *Pleurotus*
28. *Pleurotus (Pleurotellus) porrigens,* angel wings; edible. Spores white.
29. *Pleurotus (Panellus) serotinus,* oyster mushroom; edible. Spores white.

Genus *Russula*
30. *Russula aeruginea;* edible. Spores white or creamy white.
31. *Russula brevipes;* edible. Spores white.
32. *Russula claroflava (flava),* yellow russula; edible. Spores pale yellow.
33. *Russula densifolia;* edible. Spores white.
34. *Russula emetica,* emetic russula; inedible and dangerous; may be poisonous. Spores white.
35. *Russula foetens,* fetid russula; inedible and dangerous; may be poisonous. Spores white.
36. *Russula xerampelina,* woodland russula; edible. Spores pale yellow.

Genus *Tricholoma*

37. *Tricholoma aurantium;* edibility unknown. Spores white.
38. *Tricholoma flavovirens,* man on horseback; edible. Spores white.
39. *Tricholoma imbricatum,* brick top or shingled tricholoma; edibility unknown. Spores white.
40. *Tricholoma sulphureum,* sulphur tricholoma; inedible and dangerous. Spores white.
41. *Tricholoma terreum,* gray agaric, earth-colored tricholoma; edible. Spores white.

CHECK LIST OF GILLED MUSHROOMS— FAMILY AGARICACEAE—WITH SPORES NOT COLORLESS, WHITE, CREAM, YELLOW OR BUFF
Species 42 through 66

Genus *Clitopilus*
42. *Clitopilus prunulus,* plum agaric; edible. Spores pink.

Genus *Pluteus*
43. *Pluteus cervinus,* deer mushroom, fawn-colored agaric; edible. Spores pink or brownish salmon.

Genus *Cortinarius*
44. *Cortinarius cinnamomeus,* cinnamon cortinarius; edible with caution. Spores yellow-brown (rusty).
45. *Cortinarius collinitus;* edible. Spores yellow-brown (rusty).
46. *Cortinarius semisanguineus;* edibility unknown; probably edible. Spores yellow-brown (rusty).
47. *Cortinarius traganus;* edibility unknown. Spores yellow-brown (rusty).
48. *Cortinarius violaceus,* violet cortinarius; edible. Spores yellow-brown (rusty).

Genus *Gomphus (Neurophyllum)*
49. *Gomphus clavatus (Neurophyllum clavatum),* clustered chantarelle; edible when young. Spores pale ocher or yellowish orange.

Genus *Inocybe*
50. *Inocybe lacera;* poisonous. Spores yellow-brown.

Genus *Paxillus*
51. *Paxillus involutus,* involute paxillus; edible, but not recommended. Spores yellow-brown.

Genus *Pholiota*
52. *Pholiota aurea,* golden pholiota; edibility questionable; edible for some persons, but not all. Spores yellow-brown.
53. *Pholiota (Kuehneromyces) mutabilis;* edible. Spores yellow-brown.
54. *Pholiota squarrosa,* rough or scaly pholiota; edible. Spores yellow-brown.
55. *Pholiota squarroso-adiposa,* fat pholiota; edible. Spores yellow-brown.

Genus *Agaricus*
56. *Agaricus arvensis,* prairie or horse mushroom; edible. Spores purple-brown.
57. *Agaricus campestris,* meadow mushroom; edible. Spores purple-brown.
58. *Agaricus meleagris (placomyces),* scaly flat-top; edible with caution. Spores purple-brown.
59. *Agaricus silvaticus,* woodland agaric; edible with caution. Spores purple-brown.

Genus *Naematoloma*
60. *Naematoloma capnoides,* smoky-gilled woodlover; edible. Spores purple-brown.

Genus *Stropharia*
61. *Stropharia magnivelaris;* edibility unknown. Spores purple-brown.

Genus *Rozites (Pholiota)*
62. *Rozites (Pholiota) caperata,* gypsy mushroom; edible. Spores brown.

Genus *Coprinus*
63. *Coprinus atramentarius,* inky cap; edible with caution. Spores black.
64. *Coprinus comatus,* shaggy mane, lawyer's wig; edible. Spores black.
65. *Coprinus micaceus,* shining inky cap; edible. Spores black.

Genus *Gomphidius*
66. *Gomphidius glutinosus;* edible. Spores black.

CHECK LIST OF MUSHROOMS WITHOUT GILLS
Species 67 through 101

FLESHY PORE FUNGI, FAMILY *BOLETACEAE:*
(Spores either olive-brown or brown)

Genus *Boletus*
 67. *Boletus edulis,* king bolete, cep, steinpilz; edible. Spores olive-brown.
 68. *Boletus erythropus;* edible. Spores olive-brown.
 69. *Boletus mirabilis;* edible. Spores olive-brown.

Genus *Leccinum*
 70. *Leccinum aurantiacum,* orange bolete; edible. Spores olive-brown.
 71. *Leccinum scabrum,* rough-stemmed bolete; edible. Spores olive-brown.
 72. *Leccinum insigne,* orange bolete; edible. Spores olive-brown.

Genus *Suillus* (*Boletinus*)
 73. *Suillus* (*Boletinus*) *cavipes;* edible. Spores brown.

WOODY PORE FUNGI, FAMILY *POLYPORACEAE:*
(Spores white)

Genus *Caloporus* (*Polyporus*)
 74. *Caloporus* (*Polyporus*) *ovinus,* (*Albatrellus ovinus, Scutiger ovinus*), sheep polypore; edible. Spores white.

Genus *Laetiporus* (*Polyporus*)
 75. *Laetiporus* (*Polyporus*) *sulphureus,* sulphur shelf, chicken of the woods; edible. Spores white.

Genus *Polyporus*
 76. *Polyporus* (*Piptoporus*) *betulinus,* birch polypore; edibility unknown, but questionable. Spores probably white to yellowish.
 77. *Polyporus* (*Polystictus*) *versicolor;* edibility unknown. Spores white.

TOOTHED, OR HEDGEHOG, FUNGI, FAMILY *HYDNACEAE:*
(Spores either colorless, white or brownish)

Genus *Dentinum* (*Hydnum*)
 78. *Dentinum* (*Hydnum*) *repandum,* spreading hedgehog; edible. Spores white.

Genus *Hericium*
  79. *Hericium laciniatum;* edible. Spores colorless, white in mass.

Genus *Hydnum*
  80. *Hydnum imbricatum,* brick top or scaly hydnum; edible. Spores brownish.
  81. *Hydnum fennicum,* bitter hydnum; edibility questionable—edible but bitter. Spores brownish.

CLUB, OR CORAL, FUNGI, FAMILY *CLAVARIACEAE:*
(Spores varying from whitish yellow to yellow-buff-brown to ochraceous)

Genus *Ramaria (Clavaria)*
  82. *Ramaria (Clavaria) rufescens;* edible. Spores yellow-brown.
  83. *Ramaria (Clavaria) flava,* golden coral; edible. Spores yellow-buff.

Genus *Clavicorona (Clavaria)*
  84. *Clavaria cristata,* edible. Spores white to yellowish buff.
  85. *Clavicorona (Clavaria) pyxidata,* edible. Spores white to yellowish buff.

Genus *Clavariadelphus*
  86. *Clavariadelphus pistillaris;* edible. Spores whitish to buff.
  87. *Clavariadelphus sachaliensis;* edibility unknown. Spores ochraceous.
  88. *Clavariadelphus truncatus;* edible. Spores ochraceous.

SAC, OR SPONGE, FUNGI, FAMILY *HELVELLACEAE:*
(Spores whitish to yellowish)
Note: Never eat any of the *Helvellaceae* raw.

Genus *Gyromitra (Helvella)*
  89. *Gyromitra (Helvella) esculenta,* brain mushroom; poisonous. Spores yellowish.

Genus *Helvella*
  90. *Helvella infula,* hooded helvella; poisonous. Spores whitish.
  91. *Helvella lacunosa,* elfin saddle; edible, but dangerous. Spores whitish.

Genus *Morchella*
  92. *Morchella angusticeps,* conic morel; edible. Spores yellowish.
  93. *Morchella esculenta,* sponge morel; edible. Spores yellowish.

Genus *Verpa*
94. *Verpa bohemica,* false morel; inedible for some persons. Spores pale yellow.

PUFFBALLS, OR STOMACH FUNGI, FAMILY *LYCOPERDACEAE:*
(Spores olive-brown)

Genus *Calvatia*
95. *Calvatia gigantea,* giant puffball; edible. Spores olive-brown.

Genus *Lycoperdon*
96. *Lycoperdon perlatum,* gem-studded puffball; edible. Spore olive-brown.
97. *Lycoperdon pyriforme,* pear-shaped puffball; edible. Spores olive-brown.

CUP FUNGI, FAMILY *PEZIZACEAE:*
(Spore color unknown)

Genus *Peziza*
98. *Peziza badio-confusa,* pig's ears fungus; edible. Spore color unknown.
99. *Peziza repanda,* brownie cup; edible. Spore color unknown.

Genus *Aleuria*
100. *Aleuria (Peziza) aurantia,* orange peel fungus; edible. Spore color unknown.

EARTH TONGUES, FAMILY *GEOGLOSSACEAE:*
(Spore color unknown)

Genus *Spathularia*
101. *Spathularia flavida (clavata),* yellow earth tongue; edible. Spore color unknown.

Glossary

Aberrant—Differing in form from the normal character.
Abnormal—Not properly developed.
Abortive—Not perfect, or entirely lacking.
Accumbent—Lying against.
Acrid—Sharp or biting to the tongue, peppery.
Adnate—Broadly attached, as by nearly the entire length or width.
Adnexed—Narrowly attached.
Agaric—One of the gill-bearing fungi; a mushroom.
Annulus—The ring found on the stem of some mushrooms, resulting from the loosening of the inner or partial veil from the margin of the cap.
Apex—Apical end. The end farthest from the base or point of attachment.
Astringent—Puckery to the taste.
Attenuate—Becoming gradually narrower or smaller.
Base—Opposite apex. The end nearest to the point of attachment.
Buff—A light, dull brownish yellow, about the color of chamois.
Bulbous—A bulblike swelling at the base of a stem.
Button—A very young mushroom.
Caespitose—Growing in tufts or clumps, but not grown together.
Campanulate—Bell-shaped.

Cap—The pileus of a mushroom, usually at the apex of the stem.
Cartilaginous—Tough, brittle; breaking with a snap.
Ciliate—Fringed with hairs.
Clavate—Club-shaped.
Concentric—Rings or zones within one another in a series.
Convex—Regularly rounded, a half sphere.
Convolute—Brainlike lobes, folds and depressions.
Cortina—The cobwebby veil found in some mushrooms.
Cuticle—A skinlike layer.
Decurrent—(Of gills and tubes), running down the stem.
Decurved—Bent down.
Deliquescing—Dissolving into a liquid.
Depressed—Sunk below the margin.
Disk—The central part of the upper surface of a mushroom cap.
Distant—Far apart.
Emarginate—(Of gills), notched near the stem.
Equal—Uniform in length, thickness, etc.
Evanescent—Soon disappearing.
Excentric—Off-center.
Expanded—Spread out.
Farinaceous—Resembling fresh meal in odor or taste.
Fetid—Stinking.

Fibrillose—Covered with or composed of thin threadlike filaments or fibrils.
Fibrous—Covered with or composed of fibers.
Flaccid—Soft and limber, without firmness.
Flesh—The inner substance of a mushroom.
Fleshy—Composed of juicy succulent tissue.
Floccose—Cottony to woolly.
Free—Not attached.
Furfuraceous—Branlike particles, scurfy.
Genus—The major subdivision of a family or subfamily, usually consisting of more than one species.
Glabrous—Smooth, lacking of scales, hairs, etc.
Globose—Spherical, round.
Gluten—A viscous substance found on the surface of some mushrooms.
Glutinous—Very sticky, gluelike.
Granulose—Covered with granules, grainlike.
Habit—The manner of growth of a mushroom.
Habitat—The natural place of growth of a mushroom.
Homogeneous—Alike in structure and appearance.
Hyaline—Colorless, transparent.
Hygrophanous—A watery appearance when moist, changing color when dry.
Imbricate—Overlapping, shinglelike.
Infundibuliform—Funnel-shaped.
Intervenose—With veins between.
Involute—Inrolled.
Lacerate—Appearing as if torn.
Lamellae—Gills on the underside of a mushroom cap.
Latex—The milky juice found in some mushrooms.
Livid—The color of a blue-black bruise.
Lobed—Large round divisions.
Membranous—Thin and pliant.
Mycelium—The vegetative part of a fungus.
Mycology—The scientific study of the fungi.
Mycophagist—One who eats mushrooms.
Ochraceous—Light yellow color with a tinge of brown.
Ovoid—Egg-shaped.
Pallid—A pale whitish appearance.
Parasite—Any organism deriving its nourishment from another living organism, but generally giving nothing in return.
Pedicel—A slender stem.
Pellicle—A skinlike covering, the peel.
Pendulous—Hanging down.
Peridium—The outer skinlike layer of a puffball.
Persistent—Enduring or continuing.
Pileus—The same as cap.
Pith—A central stuffing in some stems.
Pore—The mouth of a tube (sometimes the same as a tube).
Poroid—Becoming joined by cross-veins as to resemble pores.
Pubescent—Covering of short, soft, downy hairs.
Pulverulent—Powdery.
Pyriform—Pear-shaped.
Reticulate—A network of lines or ridges.
Rimose—Cracked.
Rufous—Dull red (Venetian red).
Rugose—Coarsely wrinkled.
Rugulose—Finely wrinkled.
Sapid—Agreeable to the taste.
Scabrous—Rough, with short rigid projections.
Serrate—Sawtoothed.
Sessile—Lacking a stem.
Sinuate—Wavy or notched near the stem.
Species—The major subdivision of a genus or subgenus, composed of related individuals that resemble one another, are able to reproduce among themselves, but are not able to reproduce with members of another species.
Sphagnum—Soft moss, frequently found on the surface of bogs.
Spore—The reproductive body of a fungus (analogous to seed in higher plants).
Squamulose—Covered with small scales.
Squarrose—Covered with erect recurved scales.
Stalk/stipe—The stem of a mushroom.
Stipitate—Possessing a stem.
Striate—Marked with lines or furrows.
Stuffed—(Of stems), having a central spongy pith that may disappear leaving the stem hollow.
Torminose—Densely matted with a covering of soft hairs.
Toxic—Poisonous.
Truncate—Ending abruptly.
Tubaeform—Trumpet-shaped.
Tube—Same as pore.
Umbilicate—A navellike depression.
Umbo—A raised knob in the center of a mushroom cap.
Umbonate—Having an umbo.
Undulate—Wavy.
Veil—Partial, forming a ring on the stem, or universal (volva) enclosing the whole plant.
Violaceous—Violet color.
Viscid—Sticky to the touch.
Volva—That part of the universal veil that remains at the base of the stem.
Zonate—Concentric bands of different colors than the cap.

Bibliography

The following books and pamphlets may be of some use as references to enhance your knowledge of the world of the fungi. Most are currently available from many book distributors. Some are technical texts that are best used by professional mycologists, but most are suitable for field use by the amateur mushroom hunter.

Charles, Vera K., *Some Common Mushrooms and How to Know Them*, U.S. Department of Agriculture, Circular 143, 1953.

Christensen, C. M., *Common Edible Mushrooms*, The University of Minnesota Press, Minneapolis, 1947.

Christensen, C. M., *Common Fleshy Fungi*, Burgess Publishing Co., Minneapolis, Minnesota, 1959.

Composition of Foods. Agriculture Handbook No. 8, U.S. Department of Agriculture, Government Printing Office, Washington, D.C., 1963.

Food Values of Portions Commonly Used, Bowes and Church, 11th edition, revised by Charles F. Church and Helen Nichols Church, J.B. Lippincott Co., Philadelphia, 1970.

Groves, J. Walton, *Edible and Poisonous Mushrooms of Canada*, Roger Duhamel, Publisher, Ottawa, Ontario, Canada, 1962.

Harper, H. A., *Review of Physiological Chemistry*, Lange Medical Publications, Los Altos, California, 1973.

Krieger, Louis, C. C., *The Mushroom Handbook*, Dover Publications Inc., New York, 1967.

Lange, Morton, and F. Bayard Hora, *A Guide to Mushrooms and Toadstools*, E. P. Dutton & Co., New York, 1972.

McCance, R. A., and E. M. Widdowson, *Chemical Composition of Foods*, Chemical Publishing Co., Brooklyn, New York, 1947.

McKenny, Margaret, *The Savory Wild Mushroom*, University of Washington Press, Seattle, Washington, 1962.

Miller, Orson K., *Mushrooms of North America*, E. P. Dutton & Co., Inc., New York, 1972.

Orr, Robert T., and Dorothy B. Orr, *Mushrooms and Other Common Fungi of the San Francisco Bay Region*, California Natural History Guides: 8, University of California Press, Berkeley and Los Angeles, California, 1962.

Orr, Robert T., and Dorothy B. Orr, *Mushrooms and Other Common Fungi of Southern California*, California Natural History Guides: 22, University of California Press, Berkeley and Los Angeles, California, 1963.

Renaldi, Augusto, and Vassili Tyndalo, *The Complete Book of Mushrooms*, Crown Publishers, Inc., New York, 1974.

Robinson, Radcliffe F., "Food Production by Fungi," *Scientific Monthly*, vol. 75, Jan-June 1952, pp. 149-154, American Association for the Advancement of Science, Washington, D.C.

Singer, Rolf, *Mushrooms & Truffles*, Leonard Hill (Book) Ltd., London, 1961.

Smith, Alexander H., *The Mushroom Hunter's Field Guide*, University of Michigan Press, Ann Arbor, Michigan, 1971.

Talley, Manila D., "Fun with Mushrooms," *Alaska Sportsman®*, September 1968, p. 27.

Thomas, W. S., *Field Book of Common Mushrooms*, C. P. Putnam's Sons, New York, 1948.

Tosco, Umberto, and Annalaurs Fanelli, *Color Treasury of Mushrooms & Toadstools*, Crown Publishers, Inc., New York, 1972.

Von Frieden, Lucius, *Mushrooms of the World*, Bobbs-Merrill Co., New York and Indianapolis, 1969.

Wakefield, E. M., *The Observers Book of Common Fungi*, Frederick Warne & Co., Ltd., London and New York, 1958.

Wells, Virginia L., and Phyllis E. Kempton, "A Preliminary Study of Clavariadelphus in North America," *The Michigan Botanist*, vol. 7, 1968.

Wells, Virginia L., and Phyllis E. Kempton, *Know Alaska's Mushrooms*, Extension Publication No. 6, University of Alaska.

Wells, Virginia L., and Phyllis E. Kempton, "Studies on the Fleshy Fungi of Alaska I," *Lloydia*, vol. 30, no. 3, September 1967.

Wells, Virginia L., and Phyllis E. Kempton, "Studies on the Fleshy Fungi of Alaska II," *Mycologia*, vol. 60, no. 4, July-August 1968.

Index

Note: Page numbers in boldface type indicate illustrations.

A

agaric, fawn-colored, 120, 274
agaric, fly, 6, 10, 34, 36, 272
agaric, gray, 114, 274
agaric, plum, 118, 274
agaric, woodland, 152, 275
Agaricaceae, 4, 5, 14, **32,** 33, **116**-167, 269 272-275
Agaricus, **116,** 117, 146-153, 275
Agaricus arvensis, 146, 148, 275
Agaricus bisporus, 148, 243
Agaricus campestris, 146, 148, 243, 275
Agaricus meleagris (placomyces), 150, 275
Agaricus silvacola, 152
Agaricus silvaticus, 152, 275
alcohol, consumption of, 11
Aleuria, 238, 239, 278
Aleuria (Peziza) aurantia, 238, 278
Amanita, 5, 10, **32**-39, 76, 228, 232, 248, 272
Amanita (Amanitopsis) vaginata, 38, 272
Amanita bisporigera, 10
Amanita muscaria, 6, 10, 34, 36, 272
Amanita pantherina, 10
Amanita phalloides, 10
Amanita porphyria, 36, 272
amanita, purple-brown, 36, 272
Amanita tenuifolia, 10
Amanita verna, 10
Amanita virosa, 10
amanitopsis, sheathed, 38, 272
amatoxins, 9, 10
angel wings, 88, 273
annulus, 4
Armillariella (Armillaria), **32,** 33, 40, 41, 272
Armillariella (Armillaria) mellea, 40, 140, 142, 272

B

baked mushroom dishes, 259-263
Boletaceae, 4, 14, **168**-185, 269, 275, 276
bolete, 257

bolete, king, 172, 275
bolete, orange, 178, 182, 276
bolete, rough-stemmed, 180, 182, 276
Boletus, 172-177, 275, 276
Boletus edulis, 172, 275
Boletus erythropus, 174, 276
Boletus mirabilis, 176, 276
brain mushroom, 11, 216, 277
brick top hydnum, 198, 276
brick top tricholoma, 110, 274
broiled mushrooms, 259
brownie cup, 234, 236, 278

C

Caloporus (Polyporus), 186, 187, 276
Caloporus (Polyporus) ovinus, (Albatrellus ovinus, Scutiger ovinus), 186, 276
Calvatia, 228, 278
Calvatia gigantea, 228, 278
canning mushrooms, 246, 247
Cantharellus, **32,** 33, 42, 43, 132, 272
Cantharellus tubaeformis, 42, 272
cap, 5
casseroles, 259-263
Catathelasma, **32,** 33, 44, 45, 272
Catathelasma imperialis, 44, 272
cep, 172, 275
chantarelle, clustered, 132, 274
chantarelle, tubelike, 42, 272
check lists, 272-278
chicken of the woods, 186, 188, 276
Chlorophyllum molybdites, 11
Clavaria aurea, 204
Clavaria cinerea, 206
Clavaria cristata, 206, 277
Clavariaceae, 4, 14, 169-**171,** 202-214, 269, 277
Clavariadelphus, 210-214, 277
Clavariadelphus ligula, 212
Clavariadelphus pistillaris, 210, 214, 277
Clavariadelphus sachaliensis, 212, 277
Clavariadelphus truncatus, 214, 277
Clavicorona (Clavaria), 206-209, 277
Clavicorona (Clavaria) pyxidata, 208, 277

283

Clitocybe (*Lyophyllum*), **32,** 33, 42, 46-51, 78, 272
Clitocybe dealbata, 10, 46, 118
Clitocybe illudens, 46
Clitocybe multiceps (*Lyophyllum decastes*), 46, 272
Clitopilus, **116**-119, 274
Clitopilus prunulus, 118, 274
club fungi, 4, 14, 169-**171,** 202-214, 269, 277
Collybia, **32,** 33, 48, 272
Collybia acervata, 48, 272
Collybia dryophila, 50, 272
Conocybe cyanescens, 10
Conocybe cyanopus, 10
cooking with mushrooms, 247, 248
Coprinus, 11, **116,** 117, 160-165, 275
Coprinus atramentarius, 11, 160, 275
Coprinus comatus, 162, 275
Coprinus micaceus, 164, 275
coral fungi, 4, 14, 169-**171,** 202-214, 269, 277
coral, golden, 204, 277
Cortinarius, **116,** 117, 122-131, 274
Cortinarius cinnamomeus, 122, 126, 274
cortinarius, cinnamon, 122, 126, 274
Cortinarius collinitus, 124, 274
Cortinarius semisanguineus, 122, 126, 274
Cortinarius traganus, 128, 274
Cortinarius violaceus, 130, 274
cortinarius, violet, 130, 274
creamed mushrooms, 258, 259
cup fungi, 4, 14, 169-**171,** 234-239, 269, 278

D

deer mushroom, 120, 274
Dentinum (*Hydnum*), 194, 195, 276
Dentinum (*Hydnum*) *repandum,* 194, 276
drying mushrooms, 246

E

earth tongue, yellow, 240 278
earth tongues, 4, 14, 169-**171,** 240, 241, 269, 278
edibility, 270
elfin saddle, 220, 277
Entoloma lividum, 11, 46
Entoloma strictium, 11

F

false morel, 222, 226, 277
field note form, 271
Flammulina (*Collybia*), 32, 33, 52-53, 272
Flammulina (*Collybia*) *velutipes,* 52, 272
fleshy pore fungi, 4, 14, **168**-185, 269, 275, 276
food, use for, 243-268
foolproof four, 162, 188, 222, 224, 228, 230
freezing mushrooms, 245, 246
fried chicken mushroom, 46, 272
fried mushrooms, 257, 258

G

Galerina autumnalis, 10, 140
Galerina marginata, 10
Galerina venenata, 10
gastrointestinal toxins, 11, 70, 98, 100, 102
Geoglossaceae, 4, 14, 169-**171,** 240, 241, 269, 278
gilled mushrooms, 4, 5, 14, **32,** 33, **116**-167, 269, 272-275
gills, mushrooms without, 14, **168**-241, 269, 275-278
Gomphidius, **116,** 117, 166, 167, 275
Gomphidius glutinosus, 166, 275
Gomphus (*Neurophyllum*), **116,** 117, 132, 133, 274
Gomphus clavatus (*Neurophyllum clavatum*), 132, 274
gravies, 253-255
grisette, 38, 272
growth of mushroom, 3
gypsy mushroom, 158, 275
Gyromitra (*Helvella*), 11, 216, 217, 277
Gyromitra (*Helvella*) *brunnea,* 11
Gyromitra (*Helvella*) *esculenta,* 11, 216, 277
Gyromitra (*Helvella*) *fastigiata,* 11
gyromitrin, 11, 216, 218

H

Hebeloma crustuliniforme, 10, 11
hedgehog fungi, 4, 14, **168,** 169, 194-201, 269, 276
hedgehog, spreading, 194, 276
Helvella, 218-221, 277
helvella, hooded, 218, 220, 277
Helvella infula, 218, 220, 277
Helvella lacunosa, 220, 277
Helvellaceae, 4, 14, 169-**171,** 216-227, 269, 277
Hericium, 196, 197, 276
Hericium laciniatum, 196, 277
honey mushroom, 40, 140, 142, 272
hors d'oeuvres, 248, 249
horse mushroom, 146, 148, 275
Hydnaceae, 4, 14, **168,** 169, 194-201, 269, 276
Hydnum, 198-201, 277
hydnum, bitter, 200, 277
hydnum, brick top, 198, 277
Hydnum fennicum, 200, 277
Hydnum imbricatum, 198, 277
hydnum, scaly, 198, 276
Hygrophorus, **32,** 33, 42, 54-60, 272
Hygrophorus chrysodon, 56, 272
Hygrophorus conicus, 54, 272
Hygrophorus eburneus, 58, 272

I

ibotenic acid, 10
inky cap, 11, 160, 247, 275

Index 285

inky cap, shining, 164, 275
Inocybe, 10, **116**, 117, 134, 135, 274
Inocybe fastigiata, 10
Inocybe lacera, 134, 274
Inocybe napipes, 10
Inocybe patouillardi, 10

K

keys to the mushrooms, 13-31

L

Laccaria, **32**, 33, 60, 61, 272
Laccaria laccata, 60, 272
Lactarius, 11, **32**, 33, 60, 62-75, 92, 273
Lactarius controversus, 62, 273
Lactarius deliciosus, 62, 64, 273
Lactarius mucidus, 66, 273
Lactarius representaneus, 68, 273
Lactarius rufus, 11, 70, 273
Lactarius scrobiculatus, 72, 273
Lactarius torminosus, 11, 74, 273
Lactarius uvidus, 11, 68
Laetiporus (*Polyporus*), 188, 189, 276
Laetiporus (*Polyporus*) *sulphureus*, 186, 188, 276
lamellae, 5
lawyer's wig, 162, 275
Leccinum, 178-183, 276
Leccinum aurantiacum, 178, 182, 276
Leccinum insigne, 182, 276
Leccinum scabrum, 180, 182, 276
Lepiota, **32**, 33, 76, 80, 273
Lepiota clypeolaria, 76, 273
Lepiota morgani, 11
Leucopaxillus (*Clitocybe*), **32**, 33, 78, 79, 273
Leucopaxillus (*Clitocybe*) *giganteus*, 78, 273
Limacella, **32**, 33, 76, 80, 81, 273
Limacella illinita, 80, 273
Lycoperdaceae, 4, 14, 169-**171**, 228-233, 269, 278
Lycoperdon, 230-233, 278
Lycoperdon perlatum, 230, 278
Lycoperdon pyriforme, 232, 278

M

man on horseback, 108, 274
Marasmius, 11 **32**, 33, 82-85, 273
Marasmius androsaceus, 82, 273
Marasmius epiphyllus, 84, 273
Marasmius oreades, 82
Marasmius urens, 11
meadow mushroom, 146, 148, 243, 247, 275
milky cap, controversial, 62, 273
milky cap, orange, 62, 64, 273
milky cap, slimy, 66, 273
milky cap, woolly, 11, 74, 273
monomethyl hydrazine, 11, 216, 218
Morchella, 216, 222-225, 277
Morchella angusticeps, 222, 226, 277

Morchella esculenta, 224, 277
morel, conic, 222, 226, 277
morel, false, 222, 226, 277
morel, sponge, 224, 277
muscarine, 10
muscimol, 10
mushrooms without gills, 14, **168**-241, 269, 275-278
mycelium, 3
Mycena, **32**, 33, 86, 87, 273
Mycena pura, 86, 273

N

Naematoloma, **116**, 117, 154, 155, 275
Naematoloma capnoides, 154, 275
Naematoloma fasciculare, 154
nutrition, 243, 244

O

omelets, 256, 257
Omphalotus illudens, 11
orange delicious, 247
orange delight, 62, 64, 247, 273
orange peel fungus, 238, 278
oyster mushroom, 90, 273

P

Panaeolus foenisecii, 10
Paxillus, **116**, 117, 136-137, 274
paxillus, involute, 136, 274
Paxillus involutus, 136, 274
Peziza, 234-237, 278
Peziza badia, 236
Peziza badio-confusa, 234, 278
Peziza repanda, 234, 236, 278
Pezizaceae, 4, 14, 169-**171**, 234-239, 269, 278
phallotoxins, 9, 10
Pholiota, 11, **116**, 117, 138-145, 158, 275
Pholiota aurea, 11, 138, 275
pholiota, fat, 144, 275
pholiota, golden, 11, 138, 275
Pholiota (*Kuehneromyces*) *mutabilis*, 140, 275
pholiota, rough, 138, 142, 275
pholiota, scaly, 138, 142, 275
Pholiota squarrosa, 138, 142, 275
Pholiota squarroso-adiposa, 144, 275
picking mushrooms, 245
pig's ears fungus, 234, 278
Pleurotus, **32**, 33, 88-91, 273
Pleurotus (*Panellus*) *serotinus*, 90, 273
Pleurotus (*Pleurotellus*) *porrigens*, 88, 273
Pluteus, **116**, 117, 120-121, 274
Pluteus cervinus, 120, 274
poisons, 7, 9-11, 70, 98, 100, 102, 216, 218
Polyporaceae, 4, 14, **168**, 169, 186-193, 269, 276
polypore, birch, 190, 276
polypore, sheep, 186, 276

polypore, sulphur, 255
Polyporus, 190-193, 276
Polyporus (Piptoporus) betulinus, 190, 276
Polyporus (Polystictus) versicolor, 192, 276
pore fungi, 4, 14, **168**-193, 269, 275, 276
prairie mushroom, 146, 148, 275
preserving mushrooms, 245-247
psilocin, 10
Psilocybe caerulescens, 10
Psilocybe cubensis, 10
Psilocybe fimentaria, 10
Psilocybe mexicana, 10
Psilocybe semilanceata, 10
psilocybin, 10
puffball, 4, 14, 169-**171**, 228-233, 248, 251-253, 257, 269, 278
puffball, gem-studded, 230, 278
puffball, giant, 228, 278
puffball, pear-shaped, 232, 278

R

Ramaria botrytis, 202
Ramaria (Clavaria), 11, 202-205, 277
Ramaria flava, 204, 277
Ramaria formosa, 11, 202, 204
Ramaria (Clavaria) rufescens, 202, 277
recipes, 245-268
relishes, 248, 249
Rozites (Pholiota), **116**, 117, 158, 159, 275
Rozites (Pholiota) caperata, 158, 275
Russula, 11, **32,** 33, 62, 92-105, 273
Russula aeruginea, 92, 273
Russula brevipes, 94, 273
Russula claroflava (flava), 96, 273
Russula densifolia, 98, 273
russula, emetic, 11, 100, 273
Russula emetica, 11, 100, 273
russula, fetid, 102, 273
Russula foetens, 102, 273
Russula fragilis, 11
russula, woodland, 104, 273
Russula xerampelina, 104, 273
russula, yellow, 96, 273

S

sac fungi, 4, 14, 169-**171**, 216-227, 269, 277
salad dressings, 252, 253
salads, 252, 253
sandwiches, 248
Sarcodon (Hydnum), 198, 199, 276
Sarcodon (Hydnum) imbricatum, 198, 276
Sarcoscypha coccinea, 238
scaly flat-top, 150, 275
scaly pholiota, 138, 142, 275
shaggy mane, 162, 247, 248, 260, 263, 275
souffles, 256, 257
soups, 249-252
Spathularia, 240, 241, 278
Spathularia flavida (clavata), 240, 278
sponge fungi, 4, 14, 169-**171**, 216-227, 269, 277
sponge morel, 224, 277
spore color, 6, 270, 271
spore print, 6, 7
spreads, 248, 249
statistical summary, 269-271
steinpilz, 172, 275
stem, 4
stocks, 249-252
stomach fungi, 4, 14, 169-171, 228-233, 269, 278
storing mushrooms, 245, 246
Stropharia, **116,** 117, 156, 157, 275
Stropharia magnivelaris, 156, 275
structure of mushroom, 3
stuffed mushrooms, 264, 265
Suillus (Boletinus), 184, 185, 276
Suillus (Boletinus) cavipes, 184, 276
sulphur polypore, 255
sulphur shelf, 186, 188, 276

T

toadstool, 7
toothed fungi, 4, 14, **168,** 169, 194-201, 269, 276
toxins, 7, 9-11, 70, 98, 100, 102, 216, 218
Tricholoma, 11, **32,** 33, 78, 106-115, 274
Tricholoma aurantium, 106, 274
tricholoma, brick top, 110, 274
tricholoma, earth-colored, 114, 274
Tricholoma flavovirens, 108, 274
Tricholoma imbricatum, 110, 274
Tricholoma pardinum, 11
tricholoma, shingled, 110, 274
tricholoma, sulphur, 112, 274
Tricholoma sulphureum, 112, 274
Tricholoma terreum, 114, 274

V

velvet-stemmed mushroom, 52, 272
Verpa, 226-227, 277
Verpa bohemica, 222, 226, 277
volva, 4

W

waxy cap, cone-shaped, 54, 272
woodland agaric, 152, 275
woodland russula, 104, 273
woodlover, smoky-gilled, 154, 275
woods, chicken of the, 186, 188, 276
woody pore fungi, 4, 14, **168,** 169, 186-193, 269, 276